CHILDREN OF THE GREAT COUNTRY HOUSES

Also by Adeline Hartcup

ANGELICA
MORNING FACES
(with John Hartcup)
BELOW STAIRS IN THE GREAT COUNTRY HOUSES

Children of the
Great Country
Houses

ADELINE HARTCUP

SIDGWICK & JACKSON
LONDON

First published in Great Britain in 1982
by Sidgwick and Jackson Limited
Copyright © 1982 Adeline Hartcup

ISBN 0-283-98826-6

Printed in Great Britain by
Hazell Watson and Viney Ltd,
Aylesbury, Bucks
for Sidgwick and Jackson Limited
1 Tavistock Chambers, Bloomsbury Way
London WC1A 2SG
Phototypesetting by Swiftpages Limited, Liverpool

For Amelia, Imogen, Selina,
Thomas, Charles, Oliver
and (at least) one more,
this description of children
so very different from them

Contents

List of Illustrations

Acknowledgements

The great country houses still draw their crowds of visitors, interested (admiringly or grudgingly) in the way life was lived there in those very different days which it is hard to believe are only a generation or two away from our own. Plenty has been written about their history and architecture, their paintings and furniture, and about the men and women – many of them important and well-known in their time – who owned them.

But the children have been forgotten. What were they like? How did they live? Families were large then, and almost all the great houses had large, well-filled nurseries and schoolrooms tucked away – tactfully and tactically – out of earshot on the upper floors.

The door now opens on some of those rooms and corridors which once were noisy with laughter and tears, games and lessons, cuddlings and scoldings, and today stand silent, empty, unvisited and forgotten. It is on nineteenth-century families that it opens (and closes), but life and history are not neatly packaged in machine-wrapped portions, so there is a slight overlap – backwards into the end of the eighteenth century and forwards into our own times, where the picture is filled in with recollections from some of those who were children in the great houses during the reign of Edward VII and the years immediately before the First World War. Of course there were hundreds of families and children to investigate, and only those who for various reasons were short-listed have reached the printed page.

Much of my material comes fresh from family archives, where until now it has lain untapped – often because no one thought it interesting or important. But bundles of letters, diaries, and children's drawings have their tale to tell – and not only when they happen to be the first babyish scribblings of such eminent dignitaries as the sons of the third Marquess of Salisbury, or the equally touching letters that Lord Melbourne wrote to his mentally-handicapped son Augustus and to his illegitimate adopted daughter Susan.

Permission to browse in their historic family archives was kindly given to me by Lord Egremont, the Marquess of Salisbury, Lady Ravensdale and the Hon. David Lytton-Cobbold. The Hertfordshire and West Sussex Record Offices and the Kent Archives Office allowed me to use the records in their keeping. It was a pleasure as well as a great help to hear from Lady Blanche Cobbold and Lord Longford about their days in the nursery and – another, equally important side of the medal – from Miss Grace Browning about the experiences of an affectionate Nanny.

PART ONE

1

Mothers and Fathers

Throughout the ages, mothers and fathers have had an immense power for good or evil. Even the well-starched ranks of nurses, nurserymaids and governesses in the great houses of the last century still left plenty of play for parental influence. Like the three bears in the story, there were good, middling and bad parents; the good ones were close to their children, and loving; the middling ones were remote or unconcerned; the bad ones were neglectful and sometimes downright hostile. No doubt that is how it was in the beginning, is now, and forever shall be. One main difference was that in the nineteenth century it was very difficult for children to escape from their home. Parents sometimes managed to, but it will be seen that in such cases the dice were loaded heavily in the father's favour. The merest whisper of impropriety forfeited a mother's claim to her children – even to the sight of them.

Some sayings of Lord Melbourne, the Prime Minister, give a three-dimensional view of upper-class family life in his time. He told the young Queen Victoria that the measure of married happiness was to have a great number of children, and that almost everyone's character was formed by his mother, so it was mothers who should be punished if children did not turn out well. In his old age he was heard to say, as he stood looking at a portrait of his own mother: 'A remarkable woman, a devoted mother, and excellent wife – but not chaste, not chaste.' To cap it all, he said that everything useful he had ever learned had been taught him by a nurserymaid.

One way to avoid generalizations is to attempt a cross-section, so that clips of parents and children at different levels of affection and under-standing can be flashed on the screen. The loving parents deserve to come first. Among the most devoted were Charles Wood, second Viscount Halifax, and his wife Agnes, whose strong religious faith helped them when three of their four sons died within a few years. Charles must have been one of the most demonstrative as well as playful of Victorian fathers. He would swoop on the boys and their sisters in the schoolroom and take them for a ride, or a romp in the loft over the stable. He read them ghost stories and Scott's novels during the evenings, shared their pleasures and interests, and wrote them dozens of amusing and loving letters. Among the most endearing are those he wrote to his son Edward (who had the unhappy privilege of being Foreign Secretary at the outbreak of the Second World War), as if they came from his doll, Jack Tar, away in hospital with a broken leg. They told how he was gradually getting better, and finally that he would land on the coast nearby the next day. When the children went to the beach, there was Jack Tar with two sound legs, bobbing about in a boat on the waves. At other times Lord Halifax's imaginative games aimed at scaring: he would pretend he was a witch, stage a 'gypsy raid' to capture a small boy, or creep around in soundless felt shoes to jump suddenly out on the children.

Though most of the disciplining was done by their mother, he could be firm at times, though he never beat his children. After a serious talking-to he would say: 'Come now, that is forgotten. Give me a kiss.' Both parents were sympathetic and supportive to Edward, who had been born with an atrophied, handless left arm. His father was unusually uninhibited in expressing his affection. A birthday letter ended: 'Goodbye my own darling. I love you with all my heart.' When Edward's brothers died, his father's affection must have been almost overpoweringly intense. 'You do not know how precious you are in my eyes, my own dearest child', he wrote when Edward was twelve, 'my only little son left now that God has taken my other three to Himself. All my hopes and joys are bound up in you.'

Strangely enough, the very size and number of the great houses could discourage intimacy between parents and children – all the more so, of course, when fathers had political or other jobs which kept them often away from home. Hugh Lupus, later the first Duke of Westminster, spent his early childhood with seven sisters in the big nurseries at Eaton Hall and in Grosvenor Square, where they were looked after by two nurses and relays of nurserymaids. Till Hugh was seven he saw little of his parents. But then the family were given Motcombe House in Dorset as their first country home, and so moved out of the ancestral *palazzi*. Motcombe was too small for children and parents to go on living stratified lives, and Hugh's father now gave up his political career, so the family came together. Instead of separate nursery meals, the children ate *en famille* and they all spent their evenings together. They romped and played hunt the slipper, their father taught the children chess and Latin, and read aloud – a Shakespeare play, Gibbon, or a narrative poem of Scott's – while their mother did her embroidery.

But fathers in public life, even if they lived in big ancestral homes, could also be close to their children. When the second Marquess of Salisbury's wife died in 1839, he determined to follow her methods of bringing up their family. He took the children from London to Hatfield the night she died, and supervised their education himself, calling them into his dressing-room for history lessons and carefully correcting their essays. He was ahead of his times in insisting that girls too should have a good education. He also made what now seem tough demands on them. On some evenings he would come back from the House of Lords to his home in Arlington Street at eleven o'clock and wake his daughters. 'Get up and dress, girls!' he would call, and within an hour the horses would be bowling along the road to Hertfordshire. Even today, when telephones, cars and motorways have brought Hatfield within an hour or so of London, such an on-the-spur-of-the-moment upheaval would ask a lot of children who were already fast asleep in bed. In those days it must have involved waking the London household so that they could help the girls dress and pack; rousing grooms, coachman and horses; and sending an outrider ahead to get the park gates open, the Hatfield servants up, and the house ready for them. It says a lot for the lively Cecil upbringing that the girls accepted such sudden decisions with good humour and took them in their stride.

What about the loving mothers? There were plenty of these, some of them little more than children themselves when their first babies were born, so that they romped, slept and chatted with them, nursed them when they were ill, acted in amateur theatricals with them, and of course very often led their prayers, hymns and Bible readings. Was it these early marriages and the heavy responsibility for their large families that transformed so many of those light-hearted girls in twenty years or so into formidably dominating matriarchs like Lady Stanley of Alderley and her daughter Rosalind Howard?

Blanche Balfour, the mother of the future Prime Minister, A. J. Balfour, was one of the girls the second Marquess of Salisbury woke up for those late-night journeys to Hatfield. In 1856, only thirteen years after their marriage, her husband died, leaving her with eight children. She resolved to be both father and mother to them, shared their lives lovingly, taught them to read, and gave them their first lessons as well as her own firm religious faith. Later she read French novels to them – with judicious skipping. Brilliant and entertaining, she had an extraordinary power over her children. Her daughter told how she made her children long for her praise and attention, and commanded instant obedience. 'You felt you had to do right when with her', she wrote, and as a birthday present she could imagine no more delicious treat than 'a long walk alone' with her mother. Years afterwards, another daughter was asked by one of Blanche Balfour's grandchildren what she would have thought of them all. 'It is quite impossible to tell you that,' she answered. 'If any of you had known her you would all have been so different from what you are that I really cannot say.'

Such mothers, as Shakespeare did not quite say, are dangerous. Four of Blanche Balfour's children – the Prime Minister, another cabinet minister, the second Principal of Newnham College, and a Cambridge professor – were outstandingly successful. The other four – including a gambler and forger, an alcoholic, and a petty-minded old maid – were not.

There were plenty of bad parents too. Society marriages then were often 'arranged' affairs, and many of the partners found it difficult or unnecessary to love the children they had by a spouse they disliked. Byron described his mother as his 'tormentor'. When she scolded him she used to say, 'Ah, you little dog, you are a Byron all over; you are as bad as your father!' (Yet at the same time she told him he should be proud of his birth.) He wrote to his half-sister Augusta that his mother 'flies into a fit of phrenzy. . .rakes up the ashes of my *father*, abuses him, says I shall be a true Byrrone, which is the worst epithet she can invent. Am I to call this women mother?. . .I owe her respect as a Son, But I renounce her as a Friend. . .I have not told you all nor can I.' He was not yet four when his father died, but his memories of that time gave him 'very early a horror of matrimony, from the sight of domestic broils'.

Some parents were cruel because they were unhappy characters themselves, inescapably passing their wretchedness on to their children. The future twelfth Duke of Bedford had to stand in a corner of the room while his parents breakfasted in silence – inevitably, as his father was not talkative and his mother was stone-deaf. At last the Duke would turn to his son: 'Tavistock, you may leave now', he said, and the boy's sentry-duty was over. But afterwards for over twenty years father and son never spoke to each other; and the boy took his place in a dynasty of unhappy, unbalanced men who in the nineteenth century included a hypochondriac, a recluse and a suicide, and finally he too shot himself.

The 'cycle of deprivation' may be a recent term, but the phenomenon is not new. A famous victim of it was Lord Alfred Douglas, Oscar Wilde's pernicious 'Bosie'. His father, the eighth Marquess of Queensberry, had been a quarrelsome, wild boy whom no one did much to tame or educate. A recent account of the family tells how Bosie's father spent more time hunting with his own father than in the schoolroom with his tutor, shot better than he spelt, and rode before he read. He was deeply attached to his father, whose sudden death when the boy was fourteen unexpectedly made a peer of him, and this threw him even further off balance. When Bosie was born, his parents' marriage was already tottering, war between them was declared, and all the children took their mother's part. 'He did nothing for us boys', Alfred Douglas recalled. 'When he saw us he was generally good-natured and kindly, but he never lifted a finger to teach, admonish or influence us in any direction.' His mother was possessive and pampered him, his capricious father was determined to have his own way, so Alfred Douglas's bad deeds glare, in their naughty world, like the inevitable final sentence in a game of consequences.

One son who managed to survive the parental unkindness, and so break the fatal cycle, was the philanthropist eighth Earl of Shaftesbury. He was one of nine children who were heartily disliked by their parents. In his twenties he wrote of his mother as a 'dreadful woman' with a 'fiend-warmed heart'; he told of his father venting 'malignity and horror' on the girls and of neither parent ever giving the children any affection or encouragement. They were left entirely in the charge of the servants, and for days on end went cold and hungry. Occasionally his father would shoot a question from the Catechism at his son, insisting on a word-perfect answer but not caring whether the boy understood it. As a young man Shaftesbury wrote: 'Most solemnly do I pray that no family hereafter may endure from its parents what we endured.' His dedication to philanthropy sprang from this early unkindness, from religious convictions he arrived at after the death of a kindly servant who was a very close friend to him, and from an experience he had as a schoolboy when he saw some drunken men drop a coffin they were carrying, and then start cursing and swearing. He decided then to devote his life to the welfare of the poor and friendless, and he became a loving husband and father as well as a great social reformer.

Winston Churchill had a similarly unaffectionate father, and also managed to survive childhood neglect, to be happy in his marriage and family life, and to achieve greatness. His father, Lord Randolph Churchill, son of the seventh Duke of Marlborough, had himself had a stiff, loveless childhood, and he repeated the pattern with his own sons, Winston and Jack. 'Calculated coldness' is one description of his attitude; Winston begged for his father's attention, but with no success. His father would never listen to him or consider anything he said. He was completely self-centred, and no companionship with him was possible, however eagerly and often the boys begged for it. 'I would far rather', Winston wrote, 'have been apprenticed as a bricklayer's mate, or run errands as a messenger boy, or helped my father to dress the front windows of a grocer's shop. It would have been real; it would have been natural; it would have taught me more; and I should have got to know my father, which would have been a joy to me.'

Frank Harris once asked Churchill if he ever talked politics with Randolph. 'I tried,' Churchill answered. 'He only looked with contempt at me and would not answer.' Harris asked whether Churchill had liked his father. 'He wouldn't let me,' he replied. 'He treated me as if I had been a fool; barked at me whenever I questioned him.' Churchill's aunt confirmed this when she described how their father would shoo his sons away when they came to say good morning: 'The two pairs of round eyes, peeping round the screen, longed for a kind word.' At Harrow, too, their father neglected his boys. 'You have never been to see me,' Winston wrote after more than a year there. 'I shall be awfully disappointed if you don't come.' But awfully disappointed he remained.

Churchill's mother tried to make up for her husband's shortcomings. 'I owe everything to my mother; to my father, nothing', Churchill said. His early vision of her was of 'a fairy princess: a radiant being possessed of infinite riches and power. . .She shone for me like the evening star. I loved her dearly – but at a distance.' The intimacy and love he did not get from his mother came to him, it will be seen, from his nurse, Mrs Everest. His mother neglected her sons by never providing them with the stable home they needed. But they could speak freely with her, she did not shirk scolding them, and they minded what she said. When she wrote to Churchill about his bad school report, his reply began: 'My own Mummy, I can tell you your letter cut me up very much.' They were always sure of her love and interest in them, and that was important.

Winston Churchill (right) with his brother Jack and his mother, 'a radiant being possessed of infinite riches and power . . . she shone for me like the evening star'.

Mrs Everest, Winston Churchill's nurse, who he said was his 'dearest and most intimate friend' for the first twenty years of his life.

Sir George Sitwell and his wife have been brilliantly described by their children, but this account of Victorian parents cannot leave them out. The clue to their strange treatment of their family is their own unhappy marriage. Sir George disliked any traits in his children which he could trace to his wife's family rather than his own. 'My parents were strangers to me from the moment of my birth', wrote Dame Edith. Why? Because she was a girl, did not conform to her parents' idea of beauty, and 'also showed unwelcome evidence of brains'. Their mother did not attempt to hide her preference for Osbert, who was allowed all liberties, who wandered in and out of his mother's room as he liked, and who adored her unquestioningly until the shock of the first time she lost her temper with him. The high-spot every evening was when both parents came up to Osbert's room to say goodnight to him and his mother would often return for a forbidden second visit, this time bringing with her perhaps a peach or a water-ice as well as a whiff of delicious scent and loving reassurance.

But meanwhile what was happening to Edith? Did she hear those footsteps come upstairs each evening and go to Osbert's room, while she lay in bed surrounded by just as menacing Renishaw ghosts, just as dark shadows? It is remarkable that the Sitwell parents' delight in their sons and neglect of their daughter neither caused a split between the three children nor cramped the boys' affection for their mother and father. When they grew up the trio went their own way, and the relationship between Osbert and Sir George, in particular, became more complex and acrimonious. During his childhood the chief pointer to future coolness is Osbert's serious illness when he was eleven; although he was in bed and in great distress for four months, his father never came to see him – not even from the safe distance of the bedroom doorway. Sir George's affection had its limitations: not even to cheer up his son and heir was he prepared to endanger his own health.

Children's illnesses were a test of parents' feelings in those years when it was often exhausting if not also dangerous to nurse a young patient who had a serious infection. Sometimes, as the Gladstones did, both parents shared the nursing. At Bowen's Court, in southern Ireland, they arranged things differently when nineteen-year-old Henry Bowen developed smallpox soon after coming home from his Grand Tour of Europe. His mother insisted on nursing him herself, and her husband at once took himself off with the rest of the children and almost all the servants to one of the other family houses. The sound of the wagonette,

A prestigious family portrait: in 1831 C.R. Leslie, R.A., painted three generations of Grosvenors at Grosvenor House. Hugh Lupus is seen standing close to his grandfather, the Marquess of Westminster; next to him three of his sisters are playing with their mother's parrot, let out of its cage for the occasion.

For the Sargent family portrait, Sir George and Lady Ida Sitwell bivouacked in London with Edith, Osbert and Sacheverell. They took along with them furniture, a large tapestry, an earlier family portrait, ornaments, toys, and their dog so that all could be painted.

carriage, dog-cart and luggage-carts driving off was heard in the sick-room by Henry and his mother. The boy recovered, but his mother caught the illness and died. His father stayed away, leaving Henry, still weak, alone in the house with his dead mother before at long last he came back for his wife's funeral.

The Bowens were another family who were to produce an eminent novelist, and it almost seems that children who were to become gifted writers were particularly hard to assimilate in aristocratic Victorian nurseries. Vita Sackville-West's father, Lord Sackville, was puzzled when at Knole his daughter harnessed three odd-sized dogs to her little cart, threw unwanted baby rabbits over the garden wall and from the age of twelve never stopped writing. 'I wish that Vita was more *normal*', the poor man sighed to his wife. Her mother was not much less baffled. Vita felt that she had loved her as a baby but did not care much for her as a child, telling her that she could not bear to look at her because she was so ugly. She tried to teach her daughter her own shaky moral principles. 'One must always tell the truth, darling, if one can, but not *all* the truth; *toute vérité n'est pas bonne à dire.*' Vita remembered that her father 'in his quiet way' used to put her right 'with little axioms of his own'. Yet another writer who had a similar lack of communication with his parents was the future Lord Berners. His mother once asked her husband to beat the boy for some misdeed. No, he answered, he could not be bothered. His son was probably right to feel not grateful but instead offended by his father's lack of interest in him.

The great Duke of Wellington must be the last of these Victorian parents to be sketched. His relationship with his sons, coloured by the failure of his marriage and the lack of affection in his own childhood, was full of contradictions. His delight in children's company was one of the few tastes he shared with his wife. She and the boys were devoted to each other, but she also had plenty of affection to spare for other people's children, adopting six, with whom she had very loving and happy relationships.

While the boys were still young, although their father was often away on campaigns, their affection for each other was easy and straight-forward. Douro, the older boy, whose childhood coincided with the Duke's great victories, admired Wellington and longed to be like him. His mother once described how she found him studying his portrait-bust by Nollekens. 'My Nose is *such a time a-growing*', she heard him complain. But Wellington was stern with him. Douro was asked later

26

whether his father had been kind to him during his childhood. 'No', he answered, 'he never even so much as patted me on the shoulder when I was a boy, but it was because he hated my mother.' By 1823, eight years after Waterloo, the marriage was in a bad way. Wellington was at the height of his triumph; his wife, in her late forties, looked unattractive and old for her years. Douro wrote to his mother about his changed feelings for his father. 'I once thought him the most intense disciplinarian that ever lived', he said, 'and consequently avoided and feared him.' But now he found him – no less superlatively – 'the greatest man that ever lived'; it seemed to him that Wellington knew 'exactly the way to turn me any way he likes', for he had written him a letter 'without a word of severity in the whole of those two sheets.'

Parent–children relationships are often moving pictures – in both senses – which change as the years pass. What Augustus Hare called the 'unloving awe' his sons felt at first for Wellington changed after his death to wholehearted veneration. Perhaps the least complicated fatherly feelings the Duke enjoyed were with other people's children when he was himself a grandfather. Visitors to Stratfield Saye would be disconcerted to find their eminent host on all fours with young playmates under the dinner table. In the drawing-room a cushion flung suddenly through a newspaper would be the opening skirmish in a pillow-fight which they called the Battle of Waterloo. A pocketful of shillings, hung on red (Army) and blue (Navy) ribbons, would be at the ready as awards for the heroes. In more peaceful moments the old Duke would write letters to children staying in the house, watching their delight when these were delivered by the postman.

Better late than never. Wellington was a happy father at last.

2

Mentors and Tormentors

After their mothers and fathers, next in importance to the children were the various professionals who were trained and paid to look after them. Sometimes if not often, the nurses, governesses and tutors took first place in children's lives and affections.

Especially the nurses. Many were local country girls who had started as nurserymaids at fourteen or fifteen, helping the head nurse, and seeming more like older sisters to the children. Gradually they took on the nurse's job either in the same family or with relations or friends. Some nurserymaids made a knight's move on the chess board, switching to work in the kitchen or as lady's maid. Nurses had a very responsible job and could be left in sole charge of large families for long spells while parents were away. When they were not called 'Nanny' or some other affectionate nickname, they were usually granted the courtesy title of 'Mrs', even if they were unmarried. Some were in fact married, even occasionally with children of their own tucked away out of sight. These of course they knew far less well than the children they were looking after.

The records do not tell of spinsterish or bitter nannies: it seems that women need children, not men, to make them feel fulfilled and happy. There were sad moments when at seven or so their charges passed from the protecting, playful nursery into the tougher schoolroom, and there was traditional sparring between nurses and governesses who then took over. But often new babies came along to occupy their time and thoughts until at last both nursery and schoolroom stood empty and quiet. Then they either took on the grandchildren or became dignified housekeepers; one who did this at Castle Howard after twenty-five years in the nursery was still always called 'Nurse' Gibson. When at last the time came to retire, there was often a cottage, away from the hullabaloo but within visiting distance of the new generation springing up in the old nursery, who could call in for treats, games, reminiscences and story-telling. There are touching descriptions of nannies being nursed

DUNKLEY'S

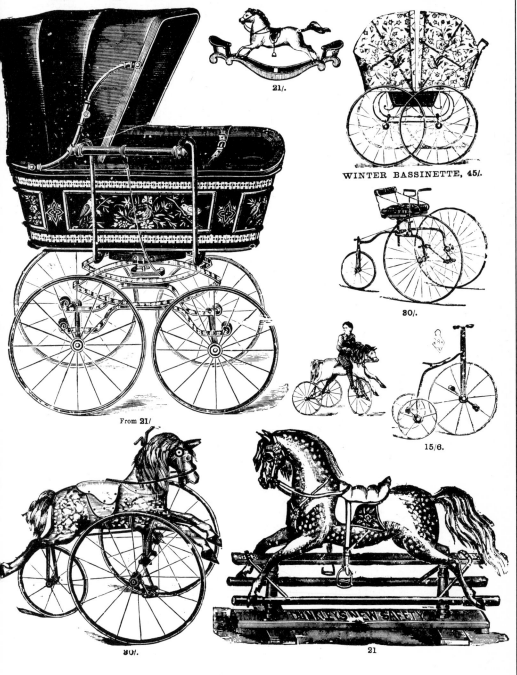

21/.

WINTER BASSINETTE, 45/.

30/.

From 21/

15/6.

30/.

21

Wheels and rockers: an advertisement showing what one firm had to offer an affluent nursery.

through their last days, like the old friends of the family they were. No national health service or geriatric ward for them.

There are surprisingly few accounts of bad nannies, though one really sadistic one victimised the future second Earl Russell until the servants alerted his mother, and she was given three hours' notice. She shook the baby when he cried, stuffed the sponge in his mouth when she washed him, gave him an empty bottle to suck, and watched while he lay screaming on the floor. Screams were good for his lungs, she said. She told the servants that she hated the child and wished him dead, but when his mother came into the room she took him in her arms and hugged him. Another baddy was Byron's pious but vicious nurse who used to have affairs with chaise-boys, and when one of these was not available went to bed with her nine-year-old charge and had sex-play with him. She also beat him when she was drunk.

But villainy was rare and unlikely to go undetected for long. There were some helpful guidelines. When there was more than one nurse, for instance, the head nurse had the honour of pushing the latest arrival's pram, while the first baby was looked after and paraded out-of-doors by her second-in-command. The second nurse had special duties: among the Petworth House papers is a letter to say that one girl was too young and not a good enough needlewoman for that job. In the grandest houses before the birth of a first baby a squad of nurses – wet, day and night – moved in, though of course the archetypal nanny was the everlasting, omniscient Comforter who presided over the whole span of a family's childhood. Governesses and tutors might (and did) come and go, but nannies were expected to go on for ever. Parents needed them as much as children did. When Lord Curzon's first wife lay dying, almost her last words begged her husband never to let their nurse leave the children. 'Give her a house at Kedleston', she managed to whisper, 'and never let her go.'

There are some lively pen-portraits of nurses. Sir Osbert Sitwell told of 'dear old Davis' in her grey alpaca dress and straw hat, with her 'usual expression of kind and puzzled patience'. She had been their mother's nurserymaid, trusted God and man implicitly (though she did not hit it off with Sir George Sitwell), had an intuitive understanding of the young and a horror of everything new, so that she wheeled her babies out in a wide antique pram, half a century older than herself. She rowed them gently on the lake, took them for Sunday afternoon walks in the Scarborough cemetery, and handed on a whole mythology of the doings

'Delightful task! to rear the tender thought,
To teach the young idea how to shoot.'
James Thomson, *The Seasons*
But not all tutors found their task delightful . . .

Out for a spin in Hyde Park, early in the present century. When there was more than one nurse, the head nurse had the honour of pushing the latest arrival's pram while an earlier baby was paraded by her second-in-command.

of her previous charges. Lady Ida Sitwell's old nurse, with whom Davis had started as nurserymaid, occasionally stayed with them. Over eighty, with strong glasses and a 'fairly heavy moustache', she always wore black in public, had to be waited upon *en princesse* and be allowed to talk without a break – usually about old times. Davis herself never achieved such glory. After a fierce confrontation with Sir George, she impulsively gave notice and – to the children's grief and probably her own surprise – it was accepted.

Events fall into odd patterns. Why ever should it be the nurses of other future writers whose faithful service was rewarded by summary dismissal? To Lady Diana Cooper the Belvoir nanny, always in black, seemed 'most lovely', though in fact she looked like a 'little dried-up monkey', never cuddled or comforted her, never let her have a toy in her pram or a doll with her in the garden. She spent seven years with the family without one holiday, and then was suddenly given notice. Vita Sackville-West, at five, also lost the nanny she loved and trusted. Why? Because three dozen quails had not arrived for a dinner-party and her mother insisted that Nanny must have eaten them.

Another nurse who was ungratefully sacked was Elizabeth Ann Everest, who Churchill said was his 'dearest and most intimate friend' during his first twenty years. She was a 'plump, friendly, forty-one-year-old widow who liked to wear dark silks and a bonnet'. It was she, he said, 'who looked after me and tended all my wants. It was to her I poured out my many troubles.' Mrs Everest remonstrated with Lady Randolph about his clothes when he was a baby, so that she wrote to her husband that nurse said 'that it was quite a disgrace how few things he has, and how shabby at that'. Everest helped Churchill learn to read, started him on arithmetic, and took him for drives and to the pantomime. Later she visited him and his brother at Harrow when their parents were too busy. 'If there be any, as I trust there are some, who rejoice that I live,' Churchill wrote later, 'to that dear and excellent woman their gratitude is due.' But she was simple and uneducated, and could not keep pace with his adult thoughts and feelings. His grandmother, the Dowager Duchess of Marlborough, always resented Mrs Everest's closeness to the Churchill boys, and in the 1890s while she was away on holiday her wages were stopped and she was dismissed. Churchill wrote indignantly to his mother about this mean treatment of one who had been her 'devoted servant for nearly twenty years' and was fonder of him and his brother than of any other people in the world. She must not be sent away, he insisted, till she had a good position to go to; Mrs Everest for her part kept up her affectionate, motherly relationship with both boys till she died.

Another endearing nurse was Mrs Gailey, who left the Duke of Norfolk's family when the Duchess became a Roman Catholic. She went to the Duke's cousin, Lady Leigh, and found her four-year-old daughter in her cot. It was not an auspicious meeting. The little girl told her that if she stayed a hundred years she would never love her as she had loved 'Brownie', her first nurse, who had left to marry the coachman. 'And if I stay a hundred years,' Mrs Gailey answered, 'I shall not love you as I did the little boys I have just left.' But after that she never looked back. The older schoolroom children always wanted to join the younger ones in the nursery after tea, when they all sat in a circle while Gailey told them fairy tales or re-told novels – including the *Pilgrim's Progress* – in her own words.

Story-telling must have been a very welcome nursery talent in those days before television. A virtuoso *raconteuse* was Mary Sheridan, who for forty years was nurse to the Persse family in Ireland. Amongst the children was the future Lady Gregory, in whose young life Mary Sheridan was the most important person. She spoke Irish, and was invaluable in that bookless house for the fairy tales and folk stories she told, laced with her own memories of Ireland, going back to the end of the eighteenth century. Lady Gregory was to acknowledge gratefully that Mary's tales of Roman Catholic folklore gave her the understanding to create Catholic peasant characters in her plays so that they appealed to audiences of either faith. The Persses were Anglo-Irish Protestants and Mary was a good Catholic; Lady Gregory remembered how 'we heretic children often said our prayers at her knee'.

The last close-up of a nurse there is room for here is Nanny Hill, who looked after Lord Arran's family in the 1870s. After their mother died, leaving four children under five, Nanny Hill slept with them all in the night-nursery of their Mayfair house. One of them later became the fourth Marchioness of Salisbury, who described how with the help of a French nurserymaid – who carried all the meals and hot water cans up the stairs, and also did all the cleaning – Nanny Hill had sole charge of the children till they were nearly grown-up. She then had her first holiday, a short visit to her old father. Lady Salisbury's earliest memories of her were when she was about thirty though the elaborate caps she wore made her look older. She was Welsh, tiny, quick-tempered, affectionate and always busy.

Perhaps a good way to bring the curtain down on nurses and their charges will be to follow Nanny Hill as she and the nurserymaid take their brood for an airing in two capacious prams. In hers, a child could lie down; the nurserymaid's was a double, victoria-shaped carriage with two seats side by side and a steering-wheel in front. It was crowned by a splendid green gingham umbrella-cum-parasol, fastened in front with a dignified bone button and hung about with a fringe of green and yellow silk. They must have been an imposing squadron as they sailed out into Hyde Park or the quiet Mayfair by-ways. If time and geography had allowed, how they would have despised those provincial Sitwells, walking through the Scarborough cemetery alongside 'dear old Davis' as she pushed little Sacheverell in a pram eighty years out-of-date.

The governess image is on the whole much chillier. Mostly refined, intelligent women though they were, theirs was not a life that would be likely to figure in a little girl's day-dreams. Many of them embarked on their career because they had not quite enough looks or dowry to land a husband; others were illegitimate daughters from 'good' families. Perhaps their very education made them feel underprivileged and unfulfilled in a way that nannies – who, after all, were in much the same boat – did not. Governesses had to be sufficiently lady-like to take their place at luncheon in the dining-room, but were not encouraged to contribute too spontaneously to the conversation; their supper was usually brought to them in the schoolroom on a tray. For about a century and a half they flourished (though that word does not suit them), their roots striking deep into good (albeit stony) Brontë soil. Their chief misfortune was to have been born then. Today they would be successful, attractive career-girls, not in the least pale or shy or sex-starved.

As it was, much depended on their employers' attitude. The letters Lady Stanley of Alderley and her daughter-in-law wrote each other in the 1840s suggest that in that household a governess's lot – like a policeman's elsewhere later – was not a happy one. When Mademoiselle R. left, Lady Stanley was glad she would not see her face again nor hear her thick voice; but she would do well for Lady W—, especially as she would not excite her jealousy; she had heard the place was 'avoided by young and respectable females'. What the children needed was 'general knowledge and a sensible woman about them who will improve their minds & be able to converse with them on what they read or see & above all one who will take an interest in them & not, like Mademoiselle R., throw them off entirely except at lessons.'

There are plenty of descriptions of grim governesses. They stood over the piano while scales were practised, with an ebony ruler at the ready to pounce on cold fingers at the first wrong note; they insisted on speaking nothing but French or German during long walks; one pulled her young charge's hair on purpose when she combed it – was it perhaps prettier than her own? – and made her write 'I am a liar and a thief' on large placards, to be displayed one on her chest and the other over her bed. Why did the mothers allow them such totalitarian powers?

At Belvoir the schoolroom was in charge of Fräulein Metzker, described by Lady Diana Cooper as 'a squat, flat-slippered, manly woman, severe and orderly, with no give, few smiles and no caresses'; after her came another Fräulein, a 'criminal type' who was dirty and had no idea of teaching. No wonder the children could not imagine why their mother had engaged her. A grotesque ex-duenna who turned up at some unusually welcoming 'reunions' to which past governesses of a Sitwell aunt were invited was 'Dicky'; she wore a wig and never stopped nagging the children. '*Taisez-vous!*' and '*Tenez-vous droits!*' she endlessly barked.

But there were amiable governesses too. Nancy Mitford's French governess was, she said, the only person who brought a civilizing influence into her childhood, and became and remained her greatest friend. She was engaged after her future pupil, then aged four, had been taken by her mother to visit Blanche, Countess of Airlie, who was horrified to hear that the child was not yet learning French. 'There is nothing so inferior', the Countess pronounced in what must surely have been a Lady Bracknell voice, 'as a gentlewoman who has no French.'

Of course tact was called for on both sides. Lady Dover left a sensitive description of how she felt when she was nervously waiting for the arrival of a new governess, who would be 'the stranger who comes among strangers', while she herself inevitably dreaded 'any change in *la manière d'être* with one's children'. But this time all was well. The new governess looked thoroughly into all the children's books, and soon their mother felt sure she had 'excellent ideas about teaching; very firm and almost strict during lessons, but very playful and good-natured in their leisure times'.

Tutors were employed to coach boys for their first boarding-schools or for Eton or Harrow, and sometimes to take on the whole education of a boy who, probably because of ill-health, was not going away to school. Many of them were clergymen who, even if they came straight from the university, needed no further qualification as teachers, and might well think a noble house as good a route as any to a comfortable living. Like the governesses, some of the most successful tutors were foreigners, who had the additional asset of being able to teach either French or German to the daughters of the family. Some seem to have been as downtrodden as the most victimised governesses. It might be expected that tutors and governesses would enjoy each other's company, perhaps to the point of falling in love and marrying, but it seems that this seldom happened. Most of those who crop up in letters, diaries and other records give the impression of not having much energy to spare for such out-of-school activities. Both parties, of course, were awkwardly short of unearned income.

To see how tutors found – and eventually lost – their jobs, it may be useful to look over the shoulder of the Rev. Edward Probert as he writes from Northumberland House in March 1869 to Lord Salisbury. He is offering his services as tutor and also – taking due care not to encroach on the rector of the parish – as chaplain. Six days later he agrees to come on January 1st next, at a stipend of £600, with a house or lodging provided; but he would like to be told where his quarters will be. He had a prompt answer, agreeing the terms, with six months' notice to be given on either side; Mr Probert will presumably want two bedrooms, two sitting-rooms and an office. After two and a half years, Lord Salisbury ended the appointment since 'you don't feel it your business to provide for the Chapel service'. It did not take long to find a replacement. The Rev. J. Lambert was told that there were three boys to prepare for Eton. At Hatfield or at Cranborne they would need only four or five hours' teaching a day; in London there would be the same lessons, but they needed more looking after as they were too young to go about alone. The terms would be the same, with a furnished house at Hatfield and lodgings in London; at Cranborne there was no separate lodging, but 'you would I dare say not object to living with us'. Mr Lambert did not object to this, nor to taking a ten-minute chapel service every morning and the afternoon service on Sundays.

In the Stanley family there was a quick turnover of four tutors in 1843 and 1844. One was sent away because he came late to breakfast, and made a mess on the carpet. It was about one of his successors that their mother wrote to her husband: 'We have had the wretched Pedagogue

'The Schoolroom Party' – a drawing by Maud Lyttelton from the illustrated family diary. One sister is being taught the three Rs while the other is improving her deportment.

In the schoolroom at Petworth: George Wyndham (born 1868) with his sister Mary, known as Tiny, his brother Charles (left) and an unnamed governess.

down some evenings but he has such a frightful imbecile manner it is only from humanity we do it.' It is not quite clear whether he was the 'Mr M' described by Lady Stanley, the children's grandmother, as 'as *safe* a man I should think as could possibly be turned into a family of girls', though she could not help thinking they would be better 'without a young man of any kind, tame in a house'. She would rather one of the girls did not learn Latin from him; that could be 'a sort of bond of intimacy' and therefore undesirable.

Some tutors were all too well qualified. Byron's daughter, Ada, Countess of Lovelace, got into deep waters when she took on Dr William Carpenter to tutor her seven-year-old son. Young and married but pompous and humourless, he was a professor at the Royal Institution and a Fellow of the Royal Society while he was with them, and he demanded full powers over the children, their governess and even their health. There was also an emotional complication, as it seems the Countess must have encouraged Dr Carpenter's attentions, and there were bad feelings when she regretted this and called him to heel.

One of the happiest appointments was that of Monsieur Drocourt, the French tutor who was also a good friend of Lord William Russell's three sons from 1832 for fourteen years. He was young, good-tempered, and ready for anything. They were living on the Continent almost all that time, and he cheerfully sat up all one night, guarding a loaded carriage as they wanted to set off early the next morning. He was equally happy to dine with Prince Metternich and with the Duke of Bedford – who called him 'little *Trop-court*' – or to spend an evening at the theatre with the boys' nurse. He learned to ride, drive and swim to keep them company, shared their enthusiasm for natural history to the point of being able to stuff a toad or a new-born puppy, and had only one holiday in eight years. His story has a happy ending: he was one of those few tutors who did marry a governess, one who came from the distinguished Metternich household. They settled in Paris, and when the boys were grown-up they never went to Paris without calling on Drocourt.

3

Privilege and Pleasure

To be one of a large family of children, based on one splendid country house and its park as well as visiting others and a London home too, must have been a good way to be young. The children usually – though not always – had plenty of company, they had roomy and beautiful surroundings indoors and out, exciting parties and festivities to punctuate the year, animals to own and look after, and toys and hobbies for every taste. The possibilities for pleasure were almost endless. To follow them, even on paper, is itself quite a spree.

Many of the houses – take Belvoir or Longleat, just as two examples – gave one family, however large or small, living-space on the scale of a well-endowed private school today. Inside, the children usually had the top floors as their kingdom; outside, they had splendid gardens and a park – often a deer-park – to enjoy, sometimes a river to fish and bathe in, home farms, stables, kennels, and game reserves to visit on foot or on ponies. Many families had their own boats and canoes, tennis courts, bowling-greens, croquet lawns, sometimes a cricket pitch and even squash courts. Some estates were so large that it took more than one day's riding to get outside them; others had unknown wild country nearby to explore. No wonder so many of the children kept their delight in 'country pleasures' all their lives.

It is difficult to choose just a few families to describe in their settings. At Inveraray Castle in Scotland, Blanche Balfour, the Duke of Argyll's grand-daughter, enjoyed driving with him in his landau along the shores of Loch Fyne and up the glens of Aray or Shira; almost every day they went on the loch in his steam-launch. They sometimes anchored and fished, or dropped a great dredge-net which brought up curious shells, giant sea-urchins and a huge conger eel. Away to the south, the Halifax family had three superb habitats: in Devon, based mainly on Powderham Castle, there were Dartmoor, the Teign valley, picnics in the heather, dizzying cliff walks, paddling and sand-castles on the beach, and fishing at sea with a boatman. They also had two Yorkshire homes, where young Edward knew 'the height of human happiness' as he rode his pony down the dales and over the moor.

In Ireland, the future Lady Gregory was surrounded by the 'wide beauty' of the hills, moors and the distant Atlantic, the trout stream with water-birds' nests and otters' caves, deer in the woods and an occasional eagle in the sky. What she enjoyed most were the activities on a six-thousand-acre working estate with its own smithy, sawmill, carpenters' workshops, coach-houses, cow-byres, dairy, laundry, pig-sties and kennels. She was to draw on these in her plays, as the Sitwells drew on Renishaw in their books. There the children's treats were drives in the pony-cart, picking wild strawberries and raspberries in the woods, donkey rides, fishing on the lake, making butter in the dairy, having tea with a farmer's wife and – by way of contrast – lakeside picnics with a camp-fire to boil the kettle which a footman brought down, as well as a well-filled hamper, at tea-time.

On the same wild and lavish scale were the picnics which were based on Chillingham Castle in Northumberland. The five young children with their parents and a friend or two drove in little basket-carriages over the park to the moors, where luncheon was brought to them in a larger carriage. After the picnic they went on down to the coast, where they scrambled on the rocks and sands, sketched, had another camp-fire and picnic tea, told stories, and then drove home through the deer-park.

Most of the fathers were keen sportsmen who encouraged their sons to shoot, fish and hunt. George Russell was not the only boy who disappointed his father. 'I abhorred shooting', he confessed, 'and was badly bored by coursing and fishing. Indeed, I believe I can say with literal truth that I have never killed anything larger than a wasp, and that only in self-defence.' For that matter, Hatfield was no nursery of sportsmen, but there too the children enjoyed chasing the deer on foot, hunting rats and rabbits – with an extra excitement when they sometimes hunted rabbits at night with a long net. Elsewhere ferreting and bat-fowling were mini-bloodsports that brought the boys from the big house and the village together, sometimes in a joint poaching foray on the ducal preserves. Archery, skating and swimming were gentler sports that the girls also enjoyed.

The English aristocracy are as well known for loving animals as their French counterparts are for loving women, and inevitably this rubbed off on the children. They had dozens of pets – dogs, cats, ponies, donkeys, rabbits and canaries, of course, but some stranger ones too.

There were tame fawns and dormice, pigeons and hawks. In 1834 the Cecil girls had silkworms at Hatfield; at Brocket, not far away, Lady Caroline Lamb, her backward son Augustus and her adopted daughter Susan kept partridges as well as a pea-hen who responded to their affection – or perhaps to a peacock's? – by laying two eggs. 'Peaky' of Renishaw was another much-loved peacock who was the object of all the four-year-old Edith Sitwell's otherwise unappreciated love. 'This love', she later wrote, 'was, at that time, returned.' His crown made Peaky a little taller than Edith, but they were almost the same height and walked round the fine Renishaw gardens together, her arm round his lovely neck. 'Other friends' of hers were a baby owl that had fallen out of its nest and a puffin whose leg had been damaged and replaced with a wooden one. Nor was that all. The Renishaw butler's brother was a fisherman, and he introduced the young Sitwells to a tame seal which followed them along the sands, poking its nose into its master's knee as it bellowed for fish. It even made one journey by train and another by cab. An animal which also delighted the Sitwell children was their grand-mother's pet monkey, who distinguished himself by swallowing an aunt's artificial hair coil, her spectacles, cap, chain and locket.

Three children who were seriously interested in natural history were Lord William Russell's sons. Among the animals they kept as pets were dogs, parakeets, hedgehogs, mice, lizards, tortoises, silkworms, snakes, toads and frogs. One of their frogs laid over two thousand eggs, which the boys tenderly carried back to what their French tutor called their 'ruisseau natal'. A girl who was always bored by toys but fascinated by living things was Frances (Daisy) Maynard, later well known as the Countess of Warwick. She watched insects and reptiles for hours on end, had toads and frogs as pets, and climbed a tall tree to observe a goldcrest's nest. She could not remember not being able to ride, and her stepfather trusted her and his own children on even the most tempera-mental of his young thoroughbreds.

No wonder toys did not seem very interesting. But other children enjoyed them, and nurseries were crowded with dolls and dolls' houses, rocking-horses and hobby-horses, guns, tops and of course toy soldiers – English and Russians at the time of the Crimean War, English and Sepoys in the days of the Indian Mutiny. Churchill spent hours ranging his soldiers on the nursery floor; when he was nine he had fifteen hundred of them, manoeuvred them into battle, requisitioned peas and pebbles as ammunition, stormed forts and bridges, and – prophetically, perhaps? – used real water to keep his enemy at bay.

What games did the children play in their stately nurseries? All the classic ones, of course – card-games like whist, beggar-my-neighbour, old maid, commerce and *écarté*; then there were chess, draughts and backgammon, and paper-games like consequences and riddles. (The Wyndham children did these in French, under pressure from a diligent tutor.) Getting more active, there were hunt-the-slipper, clumps, hide-and-seek and dumb crambo. Out of doors, as well as cricket, tennis and croquet, there were battledore-and-shuttlecock, rounders, 'flags' and diabolo (a small humming top), thrown as high as the roofs of Hatfield House and then caught on a string between sticks. One of the most amusing home-made games was played at Inveraray, when a box of photographs of the Duke of Argyll's relations and friends was found and the pictures were dealt out to the children, who played whist with them, the ugliest portrait taking the trick. Unfortunately the Duke considered this game 'unsuitable' – a very final word in his vocabulary – and banned it.

There were specially pious 'Sunday games' in some households, where scrapbooks were filled with holy texts, and descriptions of Bible scenes had to be guessed – another ploy which occasionally alerted the censor. Curiously enough, it was the virtuous Quaker Gurneys of Earlham who pulled off one of the most dramatic play-exploits when the seven children linked arms across the road and stopped the mail-coach as it galloped on its way – interesting evidence that children could stage daring deeds without the inspiration of television or Westerns. Unfortunately there is no record of adult reactions. Were the history books blamed, with their tales of violence? Or the heavy diet of morality and lessons that the (undeniably happy) Gurneys were given? Most likely there was no punishment or disapproval for what could be accepted as normal youthful high spirits.

There was plenty of time for hobbies. The children gardened, kept diaries, scrapbooks and commonplace books, sketched and painted, collected coins and stamps, made wooden animals for miniature farms and menageries, cooked jams and toffees, sewed dresses for dolls, and built twig-houses and tree-huts out of doors. Botany was one of the most serious hobbies, often because a tutor or governess set the pace. One enthusiastic solo botanist was Robert Cecil, the future third Marquess of Salisbury and Prime Minister. After his mother died and he had been very unhappy at Eton, he was brought home to work with a tutor at

The Hon. V.A. Spencer was one of the fortunate few. Not many boys had tricycles in 1869.

But most noble nurseries had a rocking-horse. This water-colour by Octavia Oakley shows an earlier generation of Sitwell children with theirs.

Hatfield. His sisters were married, his brothers away, and he spent whole days on his own in the countryside, searching for plants. He said later that this was the happiest time of his childhood. He went off dressed in old, shabby clothes and once was even arrested by a local farmer who thought the ragamuffin he had caught must be a poacher's boy. An equally dedicated naturalist was the future eighth Duke of Argyll, who during his childhood hardly ever left his remote Scottish home. His father gave him a small hand telescope, which he used to identify every bird he saw, matching it with its song and making careful notes. His own window was level with the nests of a vast rookery which he watched endlessly, noticing that one bird fed another's young, and querying whether these perhaps were orphans.

In many of the great houses there were magnificent libraries, where bookish children could browse almost as long and as contentedly as the deer in the park outside the windows. Favourite books which are often mentioned were Edward Lear's *Complete Nonsense* (written for the Stanley children at Knowsley), the novels of Captain Marryat and Rider Haggard, and Macaulay's *Lays of Ancient Rome*. When he was a boy, Churchill's favourite author was Rider Haggard; he is said to have read *King Solomon's Mines* fourteen times by the time he had had as many birthdays, and it was not much later that he could recite twelve hundred lines of the *Lays of Ancient Rome* without a slip.

The *Lays* were the first primer of another bookish child. After hearing her mother read *Horatius*, Blanche Balfour refused to listen to anything else; so after several repeat performances, her mother handed her the book. 'Read it yourself!' she said. Knowing many of the lines by heart, she soon managed this and was rewarded with a fine edition of the book for her fifth birthday. All the houses she knew then were 'full of books', and her mother chose the children's reading carefully. The books had to be 'good English' – she allowed no slang – and her list was topped by Maria Edgeworth, Mrs Molesworth and, later, Scott.

Another young reader was charmed by Macaulay at Chevening, in Kent. The ten-year-old future Earl of Rosebery had gone to the rescue of a little girl whose muslin dress had caught fire at a Christmas party, and he was badly burned. While he was convalescing his mother gave him Macaulay's *Essays* to read. His burn scars were with him all his life, but so was the memory of his reading. 'To that book I owe whatever ambitions or aspirations I have ever indulged in,' he acknowledged. 'No man can intellectually owe another more.'

Many children, it seems, remember the gift of a favourite book – particularly if it is a fine edition. Augustus Hare more than once was allowed to choose any book for himself from the Cavendish bookshelves at Compton Place. But some children resisted. One eminent future writer, publisher and father of writers – a triple literary achievement – had a *penchant* for 'trash' and magazine stories when he was a boy. In the end, Lord Longford's mother resorted to bribery, offering him ten shillings if he read *A Tale of Two Cities*, and fifteen shillings for *The Pickwick Papers*.

It is always interesting to see what presents children are given, especially if they are allowed to choose. The Stanley family's hopes for Christmas 1849 were described in a letter from their mother to their father. Johnny wanted 'a tolerable good paper knife with J.C. Stanley engraved on it. . .Alice would like a fan, an old one, she doesn't like the gaudy new ones. Blanche a tortoiseshell comb, and Lyulph any of Marryat's novels. If you cannot get Alice a fan any pretty thing would do, a statuette particularly, Algernon only wants a common whip.'

Another list of presents comes from Petworth in 1880 when the Wyndham children described what they had for their birthdays. When she was ten, Mary had a prayer book (from her mother), a letter-case (from Mademoiselle), a red satin photograph screen, a penknife, a Japanese box, a glass pyramid painted with flowers, and a china basket for flowers. For his fifth birthday her brother had a 'him book, a perse, a pen and a wauking stick'.

Not many eatables crop up in the records. Ginger and peppermint drops, barley sugar from Gunter's, sponge biscuits, ginger cake, toffee and both cowslip and ginger wine were all welcome treats, though less substantial than the books, playing-cards, dancing-shoes, bicycles and cricket jackets that are also mentioned. Animals were favourite presents, and donkeys and ponies often arrived with natty little carriages to pull. The future Lady Ottoline Morrell, when she was a girl, drove a miniature phaeton drawn by two Shetland ponies round the grounds of Welbeck Abbey; but she would have enjoyed it more if she had had a friend to share the fun. She knew no one of her own age and it was only when a cousin came to stay that the phaeton had two passengers. One very special present was given to Blanche Balfour after she was taken to see Queen Victoria at Kensington Palace. She was seven, it was 1887, the year of the Queen's Jubilee, and the next day a royal carriage delivered a splendid white dress, a present to the little girl from the Queen. Overjoyed, she said she would wear it every day. No, said her mother, she must keep it all her life but wear it very seldom. However, Jubilee Day was coming soon, and she could wear it then.

Several home pleasures came through the arts. Music, dancing and sketching were considered ladylike accomplishments, and can be seen in action, as on the evening in 1837 at Dalmeny House when Lady Rosebery played the harp, her son the 'cello and her daughter the piano. For boys, music was less of an asset. When he was young, the Duke of Wellington had loved playing the violin, but he knew that such a pastime was impossible for a soldier so he broke his fiddle in two the night before he joined the Army. The Sitwells were naturally open to the arts though Sir George characteristically thwarted Edith by denigrating her favourite poems and arranging for her to have 'cello lessons when she wanted to learn the piano.

Other artistic pleasures were enjoyed when the children were living in their London homes and were taken to Madame Tussaud's, to the famous Panorama, the British Museum, pantomimes, operas, theatres and galleries. Blanche Balfour was taken when she was thirteen by friends who knew Henry Irving and Ellen Terry to see them in Tennyson's *Becket*. At the end, Ellen Terry came to their box, still wearing her grease-paint and Fair Rosamund's white nun's habit. When she heard that it was Blanche's first play, she kissed her, took her on to the stage, and introduced her to Irving. Blanche had already had similar V.I.P. treatment at the House of Commons, where she was invited by the Speaker to sit in his Chair. She and other children with Parliamentary contacts enjoyed tea-parties with strawberries and cream on the Terrace of the House. George Russell was more seriously interested in politics. As Sergeant-at-Arms, his father got him a seat in the gallery and he never forgot the debates he heard there when the Tory Reform Bill came under fire.

Perhaps most dazzling of all the pleasures were the parties for both children and grown-ups. At Hatfield during the 1870s, about a hundred and fifty young people danced the New Year in, and in the summer there were firework parties in the vineyard. Most of the great houses had countless splendid receptions as well as celebrations for weddings, twenty-first birthdays, flower shows and cricket matches. In London there were royal parties for children at the palaces. In May 1831, just before Princess Victoria's twelfth birthday, William IV gave a Juvenile Ball to which he invited 'all the younger branches of the Nobility'. Poor

Two favourite sports. The cricketer is probably Hugh Wyndham of Petworth. The photographer's rural backcloth is not a very convincing cricket-pitch. The girl on her pony was photographed in about 1870, and perhaps was sometimes allowed to be less formally dressed when she trotted off over the cobbles.

backward Augustus Lamb probably did not enjoy it much, though from a letter written long afterwards to remind him of it we know what he wore: 'a light blue velvet Jacket with point lace collar falling over white silk waistcoat and trousers, white silk stockings, black kid shoes, and diamond buckles. You were much admired in the Ball room. You led off the Ball and danced remarkably well.'

In the great houses Christmas was always a festive occasion, with crowds of relations and friends, and hospitality for tenants, local school-children and 'the village'. The children of the family went into the kitchen to see the huge joints turning on spits before blazing fires while the kitchenmaids basted them. At the Halifax family's Christmas parties at Hickleton the gardeners brought barrowfuls of hothouse plants to decorate the dinner-table; on Christmas Eve the estate carpenter paraded the Yule log round all the bedrooms, and the children had the special treat of coming to the dinner-table for the dessert. In the dark and cold, at five o'clock on Christmas morning the waits came to sing carols round the house, and the children shivered as they held candles, by way of thanks, at the windows.

Plays were often acted at Christmas, with several performances so that all the villagers and tenants could see them. Some families had their own traditional junketings. The Leighs had a famous 'bullet pudding', a little mound of flour with a bullet at its peak: everyone had to cut a slice of the unsliceable mound, and whoever dislodged the bullet had to pick it out of the flour in his mouth. The Stanhopes had a more dramatic Christmas game – a mammoth 'Snapdragon', which involved picking raisins out of a dish of burning brandy and eating them while they were still alight.

So the privileged children had pleasures galore. But there are always some who would rather be left out, a few invitations that it is a pleasure to refuse. News of one comes in a letter to the third Marchioness of Salisbury from one of her grand-daughters. (The Cecil children still call their grandparents Goma and Gopa). It reads:

Dear Goma,
    I do not want to come to Hatfield as there is such a large Party I shall not be able to come down to dinner or play the Piano both of which I shall be able to do here. Please don't be offended.

I am your loving

Wang

Grandfather opens the the ball with a young partner. 'The Children's Party', a drawing from *The Pictorial World*, December, 1874.

Snapdragon, the Christmas game which involved picking raisins from a dish of burning brandy and eating them while they were still alight.

There is also an early note of exasperation from Sacheverell Sitwell. 'I hate these parties!' he said. 'Nothing but changing my clothes and washing my hands!'

4

Upbringing and Education

In most families the pleasures of life were the icing on a plain but nourishing cake which all the children had to eat. The ethos of their time and class condemned extravagance, vanity and frivolity, and for the most part it was agreed that inherited privilege called for willing public service in return. The children's routine was usually strenuous, often strictly disciplined and sometimes even Spartan, aimed at imprinting family values and what was considered necessary in the way of education, religion and manners. The system's success depended, of course, on the children's relationships with their parents – and with those who were employed to look after them. When these were good, children conformed and did well because they wanted to please; when relationships jarred, extreme punishments were thought up and were almost always counter-productive.

Many families had charitable traditions. At Blenheim after the midday roast the children always filled baskets with food to be taken to hard-up cottagers and villagers. Another family value was instilled by the Earl of Rosslyn, who liked his children to be straightforward about their opinions and feelings. When they were asked whether they would like the leg or the wing of a chicken, if they answered politely that they did not mind, he would say: 'All right then, you needn't have either!' He preferred them to be naughty rather than silly, and condemned shyness, maintaining that people who were shy were thinking too much of themselves. Another family insisted on children standing up as soon as grown-ups came into the room, discouraged sprawling comfortably in armchairs, and allowed jam at tea only on Sundays and one other day.

Aimed though it was at giving children a good stiff preparation for adult life, the system did not always succeed. There was an especially abrupt transition for girls who came straight from their remote and sheltered schoolrooms, unbecoming clothes and complete ignorance of sex, and found themselves – as soon as they put their hair up and 'came out' – in the amoral sybaritic whirlpool of a London season. What was expected of boys, too, was often unrelated to the realities of the outside world. The kindly Quaker Gurneys were less out of touch with ordinary life than many more aristocratic families, and yet they sent a seven-year-old boy off to school 'alone in the coach, in which there were no other passengers, to find his way to London'. At Devonshire House the irregularities of parents' lives rubbed off on the children, who at one moment were being petted and shown off in the drawing-room and then at the next were allowed to run wild in the vast house with no-one to bother about them. Caroline Lamb is said to have grown up there believing that everyone was either a duke or a beggar. From her too comes the grumble that the children could never be sure when their next meal would come, though it would certainly be served on silver.

Ethical teaching was also often inconsistent. It was all very well to tell children to be generous, but a little awkward when the friendly four-year-old Sacheverell Sitwell invited strangers to luncheon. His guests included odd-looking handicapped children and adult lunatics as well as members of the great majority whom the Sitwells called 'People At Whom You Must Not Look'. They often accepted the invitation and turned up at Renishaw. Vita Sackville-West was puzzled when her mother made her pray to God for forgiveness for a lie she had never told. At the last moment her mother changed her mind. Looking into the child's face, she said: 'Never mind, darling, perhaps we have had a little misunderstanding.' Yet it seems that she did not remonstrate when Vita stuffed her friends' nostrils with putty and flogged one small boy with stinging nettles.

The future Lord Berners was just as bewildered by his moral training. Like Bertrand Russell, he soon learned that it was a good plan to keep quiet about things he enjoyed in case they were suddenly considered immoral and thenceforth banned. When he threw his mother's spaniel out of a window to see if it would fly, she tried to beat him with a slipper – until he lost his temper and counter-attacked. He found it hard to understand why grown-ups were horrified when he swapped his toy horse for his cousin's doll. Why were music and painting considered unmasculine, when most musicians and painters had been men? Why too was it manly to kill rooks and rabbits, but not to hurt dogs or horses? When he was naughty he was told: 'If you're not careful, one of these days God will jump out from behind a cloud and catch you such a whack!' But he was not convinced. 'Nonsense!' he answered. 'God doesn't care *what* we do.'

Victorian children showed great inventiveness in the many ways they found to be naughty. Bertrand Russell dropped dead roses on the gleaming top hat of a visitor's coachman in summer, and in winter threw snowballs at him while he was driving. Throughout his long life he always enjoyed the limelight, and when he was a boy, on Sundays when Richmond Park was crowded he used to climb to the top of a tall beech tree, hang upside down and scream. When people gathered round and were about to rescue him he quietly came down to the ground. It was like Vita Sackville-West's trick of hiding in the trees and then hurling bird's eggs at the heads of the grown-ups below. At ten she was, she said, 'an unsociable and unnatural girl with long black hair and long black legs, and very short frocks and very dirty nails and torn clothes'. A third literary saboteur was Lord Berners who, after being shut in a dark cupboard as a punishment, riposted by locking the doors of all the lavatories in the house – at a time when there were visitors staying – and throwing the keys into a pond.

Other children were naughty too. Johnny Stanley was a great trial to his elders. He had a weapon he called a 'pike' – three sharp little daggers stuck into a piece of wood – and tried it out on one of the grooms, whose hand was badly hurt. He also hunted the housemaids up the stairs with his brother's spear and tore their dresses. The two boys swore and ran wild, so that the gamekeeper said he had never met such an unruly, riotous pair. Their parents were baffled by such wickedness and each put the ball in the other's court. Lady Stanley wrote to her husband: 'I shall not be sorry when you come to keep the boys in order, for they have neither the respect of children nor the good breeding of gentlemen, particularly Johnny who talks of bad French novels & altogether wants repressing.' Lord Stanley was not a helpful father. 'I am afraid neither Johnny nor Lyulph are fit to be trusted out hunting,' he wrote to his wife. 'If they get killed it will be your fault.'

A milder peccadillo is interesting mainly because it was committed by a boy who was to become an eminent churchman and statesman. The future Lord Halifax tied a girl cousin's long hair to the back of her chair, and was made to stand in penance with his pinafore over his head. When they were naughty their governess made him and the other children stand outside the schoolroom door, hoping against hope that they would be allowed back before their parents came by and saw them.

The Stanleys had only one answer to naughtiness they could not control. Lord Stanley put it in a nutshell. 'After all,' he wrote to his wife, 'the good old whipping is perhaps as good or better than anything for young boys.' Like many younger sons, Algernon Stanley was destined for the Church, and his mother thought it was his 'certain prospect of the future' at Alderley Rectory that had removed his only incentive to do any work. He had great trouble with mathematics; his grandmother judged these to be '*not* so necessary in the Church as in the Army, tho' I suppose a due portion must be flogged into him'. She had not much faith, she said, in learning being flogged into a boy, but what else could be done? Life is full of surprises: Algernon did not land up at Alderley Rectory after all. He became a Roman Catholic and eventually a bishop. Floggings were not usually inflicted on girls, though Lady Diana Cooper remembered that she and her sisters were trained by punishment only – being sent to bed for the rest of the day, having their ears boxed, and being 'dosed' with bitter rhubarb powder which they took in water, milk or jam.

Punishments were by no means the only reasons for childish unhappiness. Most parents in the last century had more than one child, but some of the only children were dreadfully lonely. Lord Acton said he had had 'no contemporaries' in his childhood, and Byron's daughter Ada also had hardly any friends. She was brought up to give unquestioning obedience to her mother, who moved restlessly round Europe. Was it because of this that, though she was athletic, for years she had what seems to have been some kind of psychosomatic paralysis and could not walk without crutches? Sudden death and succession play strange tricks on aristocratic family life; at the age of six Lady Ottoline Morrell found herself abruptly plunged into the vast rooms, wide tunnels and underground halls of Welbeck Abbey. She had no-one of her own age to play with, no companions except the servants, and no links with everyday life. She was never allowed to dress herself; everything was done for her by her maid, who combed and curled her hair, put on her clothes, tied her sashes and buckled her shoes.

There were worse troubles than loneliness. Byron felt that his 'repugnant youth', was due to his mother's '*diabolical* disposition'. Her treatment of him zigzagged between impatience, indulgence, petty scolding and insistence that he should be friendly with a neighbour who made homosexual approaches to him. He dreaded school holidays,

 is like a child sitting on the ground

 is like a swing for a child

 is like a ladder between two posts

 is like a very big ball

B

Mrs Mortimer's *Reading without Tears*, used in almost every nursery, had its own way of helping children to learn their letters.

when he had 'nothing in the world to do but play at cards and listen to the edifying conversation of old Maids'. Another who wept both at going to school and at the grim wretchedness of family life in his Grosvenor Square house and at his parents' country home was the future Lord Shaftesbury, whose only affection in his childhood came from the family housekeeper, a country girl who had been his mother's maid before her marriage. She was devoted to the boy, passed on her Evangelical faith to him, inspired deep affection as well as the philanthropical ambitions he eventually fulfilled and, dying when he was eight, left him a gold watch, telling him to wear it always and to say it was given to him by the best friend he ever had in this world.

Favouritism was another cause of children's unhappiness. Where there were titles and land to inherit, boys were of course wanted more than girls. The Sitwell parents both preferred boys to girls, though Sir George favoured his elder son while his wife doted on the younger one. Edith, five when Osbert was born, was so distressed by discovering this that she ran away – and was captured mainly because she had not yet learned to lace up her long boots. Heir favouritism – the old tradition which gave first-born males greater dignity and a larger slice of both present and future cakes – was taken for granted by the old families, doubtless just as they accepted that even the youngest had a much heftier slice of cake than most children outside the park gates. As one father wrote to his wife: 'Third sons . . . must not expect to have hunters until they can make money for themselves.'

Most children had their first lessons at home from their mother or a nurse, who taught them their letters and how to read. Lady Stanhope told how her son begged her with tears in his eyes to let him off. He would never want to be able to read, he insisted. 'But you will grow up a dunce', said his mother, 'and then you will reproach me for never having taught you.' 'Oh, never! never!' he answered – and grew up to be the eminent historian. *Reading without Tears* was the book they all started on, and only recently it was still found useful at Hatfield by the present Marchioness of Salisbury, with her children and grandchildren. Other favourites were the famous Mrs Trimmer's *History of the Robins* and *The Perambulations of a Mouse*. Mrs Trimmer also wrote children's introductions to Bible history, the Catechism, the baptism and confirmation services, and *The Charity School Spelling Book*. Maria Edgeworth's stories and educational guides were popular both with children and parents, and so was Mrs Mary Sherwood's over-moral

HISTORY

OF THE

ROBINS,

DESIGNED FOR THE

INSTRUCTION OF CHILDREN,

RESPECTING

THEIR TREATMENT OF ANIMALS.

SECOND EDITION.

DUBLIN :

PRINTED BY J. M'MULLEN, 21, DUKE-ST.

1821.

The title-page of one of the most popular of Mrs Sarah Trimmer's books for children. She
wrote nearly thirty of them, and her daughter Selina Trimmer was governess to the
Cavendish children at Chatsworth.

History of the Fairchild Family. This tells of the visit of good, god-fearing Mr and Mrs Fairchild and their children to rich Sir Charles and Lady Noble and their spoilt disobedient offspring. There is a telling comparison of the two families' behaviour, and the moral is pointed – after being very longwindedly blunted – by a dissertation from Mrs Fairchild on the evils and dangers of ambition.

Although some boys were coached at home by tutors until they were ready for their public schools, others were sent off to prep schools at a very early age. Robert Cecil was six when he went to a boarding-school near his home. It had a good reputation, but he described his life there as 'an existence among devils'. Because he was clever he was sent to Eton when he was ten, and so was in a class with boys as much as three years older than he was. 'I am bullied from morning to night', he wrote home, and was soon allowed to leave. Osbert Sitwell had an equally rough reception at his first day-school in Scarborough. The boys all went for him, shouting: 'Don't think you're everybody just because your father's a bloody baronet!' Later he went to a boarding-school, trusted by parents because it was so expensive; he found it 'a miniature model prison, essentially middle-class, with all the middle-class snobbery and love of averageness, but lacking the middle-class comforts.' But it gave him one unexpected leg-up: it was the need to tell so many lies at that school, he later decided, that started him on his career as a novelist and story-teller.

Many younger sons went off at thirteen or so to join the Navy as midshipmen. They might be sent away at once on a three-year voyage in distant and dangerous waters. The Earl of Lovelace, whose sensitive, dreamy son at that age sailed off to Van Diemen's Land with his ship in 1849, was quite unsuited to the life and eventually came to an untimely end largely because of it, tried to justify his decision to let the boy join the Navy. It was valuable, he said, for its 'discipline in education & the hardihood such a life implanted in those broken to it'. Young boys were in fact broken either to or by it. In the 1840s the qualifications for a would-be naval cadet were not over-demanding. He had to be 'in good health and fit for service, that is, free from impediment of speech, defect of vision, rupture, or other physical inefficiency. He must be able to write English from dictation, and must be acquainted with the rules of Common Arithmetic, including the Rule of Three.'

For most girls there was no question of education away from home, though at the end of the century several went to one or two exclusive day-schools when they were in London. Almost all their education was given them by governesses, with results ranging right across the spectrum. Some learned only reading, writing, Scripture and embroidery, and knew nothing of literature, science or politics. French and German were usually considered essential. Even at the beginning of this century there were strict rules at Chatsworth, where only French and German were to be spoken during the holidays, and cousins who came to stay had to toe the line. Blanche Dugdale gave her personal attention only to what she considered the most important subjects for her children – learning by heart metrical versions of certain Psalms, reading Scott's Waverley Novels, and practising the 'principles of good conversation'. There were many distinguished visitors to the house and she believed in leaving her daughter to pick up what she could from their company.

Another matriarch who, although a pioneer champion of women's education and a founder of Girton College and of girls' high schools, allowed her daughters to grow up with no grounding in science, the classics, or even English spelling and punctuation was the second Lady Stanley of Alderley. Many girls were never taught to do anything practical for themselves, like the daughter of one Scottish duke who had no idea how to sew a button on her father's coat. She was taught this useful lesson, curiously enough, by one of Queen Victoria's daughters, who married the girl's brother. The neglect of Edith Sitwell's education has been already seen to have been almost deliberate, inspired by her parents' dislike of her and by her father's strange ideas. He held that all children should spend their time on the subjects they did not enjoy and were bad at. Do at least one disagreeable thing every day, was one of his precepts, and Edith had to learn gymnastics and unfashionable dances like the Lancers. 'Nothin' a young man likes so much as a girl who's good at the parallel bars', Sir George pronounced, not altogether convincingly. Fortunately it took more than that to discourage Edith. At an early age she was asked what she was going to be when she was grown-up. Like jesting Pilate, she was not stumped for an answer. 'A genius', was her prompt reply.

But these were the deprived daughters. Many others had a very liberal home education. A letter from eleven-year-old Priscilla, the youngest of the Gurney girls, describes their life at Earlham with Quaker enthusiasm and grammar. 'Thee can't think how well we go in lessons now', she wrote. The seven girls were dressed by six o'clock, had as many lessons as possible before breakfast and then set to work, one of them reading history aloud for two hours. At present they were finding Livy 'very interesting'. They had lessons all the afternoon, then tea, a good walk, and afterwards wrote their journals till supper. Another girl who took to education as readily as her brothers took against it was Rosalind, the future Countess of Carlisle. She wrote French at five, and by ten had begun German too. At fifteen she was reading Homer, Virgil and Herodotus in translation with her governess, and was also interested in English and French literature, and the history of England, France and the ancient world. Emily Eden had a different curriculum. She said that before she was eleven she knew Boswell's *Life of Johnson*, the Memoirs of the Cardinal de Retz, Shakespeare and a great part of the Bible almost by heart. Everything, she maintained, was in those books.

While some homes overloaded their children's time, others were anxious about young minds being strained. Lord Lovelace, Byron's son-in-law, expected a lot of his nine-year-old son, with predictably disastrous results in the end. He insisted that the boy must never let his eyes stray towards the window during lessons. 'I threaten him with blinkers', he said, 'that a pair shall be taken from a nasty dirty horse & be put on him to make him look but one way.' There is no record of how he reacted to the family doctor's advice that the young Lovelaces had too little 'of absolute recreation and unbending, such as all children need'. Other fathers helped their children more gently, starting them off on Latin like Henry Streatfield who wrote endearingly to his son at his prep school, heading his letter *Henricus Henriculo suo*.

Sometimes it was a tutor who advised easier going for children who were being taken at too fast a pace. In the 1840s Mr Sockett the Petworth tutor wrote to Lady Leconfield about her eldest son George, who was something of a problem.

> He has always appeared to me, to have *little inclination* for *reading* of any kind. . .it does not seem expedient that he should have studies pressed upon him which he will only regard as *dreadful bores*, and the doing which may cause him to imbibe an unconquerable aversion for everything in the shape of a book, or the attainment of knowledge of any kind whatever, & this would be a great evil both for the present and the future.

Mr Sockett recommended that the boy should be placed with 'some very well educated, gentlemanly man, not very young – not a pedant, or book

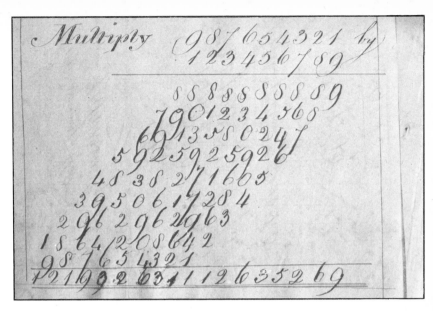

Sums had to be done without short-cuts or pocket calculators. When these two numbers were multiplied in the Petworth schoolroom they yielded an intriguing first line of figures.

'Flora glanced helplessly at her sisters, then stood hopeless before her instructress.' A familiar situation crops up in a drawing from a story book.

learned', and that with him he should visit factories in his own country, as well perhaps as galleries on the Continent.

Encouraging children to read improving books was one thing. Saving them from the perils of the printed word was, in those days, often thought to be a good idea – especially for daughters, of course. Shakespeare was not the only author to be served up often in a Bowdlerised edition. Thackeray's novels were considered too accurate a portrait of London society for young girls to read, and Byron's *Don Juan* was vetoed for at least one daughter until she was safely married. Lord Berners remembered a copy of the *Arabian Nights* which was so expurgated that it was like 'a plum-pudding without the plums'.

5

Religion and Death

Most of the great families were devout and did all they could to pass their faith on to their children. A few were indifferent or were positive disbelievers, like Sir George Sitwell who had been so tormented by religious teaching in his own boyhood that he lost all belief. Even fewer, like Bertrand Russell's parents, discarded their inherited faith after years of careful thought and enquiry. Then there were others who switched, it will be seen, to different faiths – Protestants becoming Catholics, for example, and more than one Anglican becoming a Muslim. The great majority looked forward to life after death, did not doubt that God was in his Heaven and all was right with the world, and had no grumbles about doing their duty in that state of life unto which it had pleased God to call them. Illness, pain and death were accepted as parts of the divine blueprint, signposts to the salvation of the soul. Children who did not inherit their faith from their parents were often given it by some affectionate and pious nurse or servant.

Daily prayers and Sunday church were the backbone of family religion. Prayers were usually read by the paterfamilias or a visiting clergyman, with children and staff seated in rows facing them in the drawing-room or library. In great houses like Hatfield and Castle Howard where there was a chapel, the daily service was conducted by a chaplain, who was often the boys' tutor. Sometimes it was an over-solemn, tedious occasion; sometimes it was lively and even jolly, as at Garrowby where Lady Halifax played the harmonium, her son's voice always a bar ahead of her, and he and her husband came along in rough country tweeds.

At Chatsworth at the beginning of the twentieth century the Duke of Devonshire read the daily prayers to the whole household – including a Roman Catholic butler. One of the children accompanied the hymn, which they would all choose and then mischievously stop singing at the highest notes to expose their unfortunate governess in a squeaky solo. One of the most humorous accounts of family prayers comes from Lord

Berners, who tells of the ill-feeling aroused in the servants at having to stop work, tidy themselves and spend twenty minutes on hard benches while his grandmother declaimed 'scriptural exhortations in a voice that seemed to hold out very little hope of salvation for the lower classes'. Lord Berners did his best to make the solemn-faced servants explode in guffaws of laughter, and his grandmother unintentionally co-operated as she grew older by lacing the pious occasion with exhilarating spoonerisms and other enjoyable slips of the tongue.

George Russell, the sixth Duke of Bedford's grandson, also tells of family prayers with his father reading a chapter of the Bible 'very much as the fancy took him, or where the Bible opened of itself'. When he was very young he assumed that 'the passages of the Old Testament which were read at prayers had no meaning, and that the public reading of the words, without reference to sense, was an act of piety'. Not a bad starting-point, perhaps – though not at all what was intended – for an enquiring mind. As soon as the young Russells could talk, they learned hymns by heart. No one seems to have thought of choosing those that might appeal – or even be comprehensible – to young children. 'When rising from the bed of death', the little Russells piped, as well as 'Rock of ages, cleft for me' and 'Jesu, lover of my soul'.

Sundays were very special days. The 'Duke's Pew' in the parish church had its own entrance with high walls, thick curtains, a fireplace, log basket, armchairs and large table. Round the walls of a similar one the Earl of Arran's grandchildren used to sit. Between breakfast and church their governess read to them while they painted texts or made little flower-holders for the hospital. The service was very long, with a sermon lasting half-an-hour. A moment they enjoyed was when Arthur stood on his hassock and dropped his penny resonantly into the plate from his mouth. Ordinary books were taboo on Sundays; reading had to be of religious story-books or accounts of life in the Holy Land. After tea the children's grandmother read them a sermon, which again was enlivened by an uncle who stood behind the old lady, making crazy faces. It must have been welcome when he succeeded, as they were brought up to see life as a vale of tears, followed almost certainly by eternal punishment. One year Alice spent fourteen shillings of her birthday money on a new head for her doll, with shoes and stockings for it to wear too. But her father brought her down to earth. 'Do you know, Alice,' he said, 'that is what a labourer keeps his family on for a week?'

An unusually happy picture of children's church-going comes from

Lord Berners, aged eight. An unusual photograph of an unusual boy. He did his best to make the solemn-faced servants laugh during family prayers.

Elizabeth Bowen's account of her Protestant Irish family at Bowen's Court. There were always a lot of children at church on Sunday mornings in summer. The girls came in white muslin dresses and starched white muslin hats, the smaller boys in sailor suits. In Scotland, the ladies of Lord Rosslyn's party wore satin and jewels as they drove to church with the children by carriage, while the men walked there across the park. On Sundays there were both morning and evening services, with what seemed to the children endless collects, hymns and prayers. Scottish preachers may have been specially long-winded, as at least one family let the children slip out of the private door of the pew before the sermon got under way. Families who moved between Scotland and England took part in services in both churches – an unusually broadening advantage in those non-ecumenical days. Also different were the Quaker meetings the Gurneys went to in Norwich. The Meeting House in Goat's Lane was known as 'Goat's', and they did not think much of it. A thirteen-year-old daughter wrote in her journal of 'the common run of disagreeable Quaker preachers', and admitted that she was 'always happy to escape from the claws of "Goat's"'. They could do better themselves. One evening when Prince William Frederick was visiting Earlham, they all went up to Betsy – who was to be the great prison reformer, Elizabeth Fry – in her room, and one of the sisters at the Prince's request preached them all 'a capital sermon'.

Sectarian divisions loomed large, splitting families and servants into tractarians, unitarians, methodists, presbyterians and evangelicals as well as into the broader groups of Protestants, Anglo-Catholics and Roman Catholics. Tolerance levels varied. In Ireland, where the conflict raged most fiercely, Lady Gregory remembered the children loving the little Protestant church with its large square pews for the squires' families and plain benches for villagers, gamekeepers and police. They were 'most of them Dissenters, but in Ireland a Protestant is a Protestant, all sects join hands in face of the common foe'. Yet her family had a staunch Roman Catholic as its children's nurse for forty years. Other parents were more dogmatic. The Duchess of Beaufort had such strict evangelical principles that she never allowed her eight daughters to dance or go to the theatre; yet they managed to find eight husbands who all shared their minority ideas. Sticking to principles could be hard. The Lovelaces were unitarians, even refusing to have one of their sons baptised because this would be in the name of the Father, the Son and the Holy Ghost. They searched in vain for a school, suitable

66

for 'noblemen's sons', where religious teaching left out any mention of the Trinity, and finally appointed a unitarian tutor – with consequences, it will be seen, that they came to regret.

One remarkable marriage cut across religious divisions. In 1878 the fifth Earl of Rosebery became engaged to Hannah, the only child of Baron (of the Austrian Empire) Meyer de Rothschild, of the famous Jewish banking family. Both were deeply in love, very religious and enormously wealthy. Lord Rosebery read the Bible with the children every day, often with prayers and a sermon too. He impressed them with his respect for his wife's faith, and they always remembered him taking her meal on a tray to her bedroom to end her annual fast when the Day of Atonement came to an end. When Hannah died, Lord Rosebery asked Catherine Gladstone, a close friend of theirs, to stay with his young children while he and Gladstone went to the funeral. She prayed with them in their schoolroom and admired the fine wording of the Jewish burial service. Arthur Balfour was another devout Christian who passed on to his nieces and nephews – he had no children of his own – his view that 'Christian religion and civilization owe to Judaism an immeasurable debt, strangely ill repaid'. He did what he could to repay that debt.

When parents changed their religion, complications often followed. Vita Sackville-West's mother was excommunicated for refusing to bring up her children as Roman Catholics. When the Anglican Duchess of Norfolk went over to her husband's Roman Catholicism – taking the children with her – their devoted nurse did not, and so had to leave. There was another painful split of children from the nurse they loved when the seventh Marquess of Queensberry's widow became a Roman Catholic, and her Scottish Presbyterian mother-in-law tried to take the family away from her.

Splendid church ceremonies rewarded children for their long hours of religious preparation at home. Boys took part in Queen Victoria's Coronation Service as pages to their fathers or their fathers' friends; girls were confirmed by the Archbishop of Canterbury. When he received the Duke of Hamilton's little daughter into the Church, she was four years old. To keep her quiet he had the happy idea of giving her a sugared almond to suck; but when he lifted her up, she took it from her mouth and dropped it in his. With neither hand free, there was nothing he could do, and the congregation, worried by his silence, thought he must have had a stroke.

Religious training had its practical side. George Russell tells how his family sent the children to take dinners to cottagers who were old, ill or poor. They also went to read the Bible or hymns to those who were blind or could not read. When they were old enough, they taught local children in Sunday School, and took Bible classes and prayer meetings. They were expected to save their pocket-money for the 'missionary box' or another good cause, but inevitably there were lapses. When George won a few shillings at 'the Race-Game', these were confiscated and given on his behalf to the Church Missionary Society. An aunt was inspired by the incident to write some verses for the children:

> Would you like to be told the best use for a penny?
> I can tell you a use which is better than any —
> Not on toys or on fruit or on sweetmeats to spend it,
> But over the seas to the heathen to send it.

Autres temps, autres mœurs. . .

It is important to remember the constant presence of death alongside religion during the last century. Mothers died after too many pregnancies; children died from illnesses that are no longer dangerous. Parents expected to have large families, whether they wanted these or not, and everyone accepted that several children would probably die young. Caroline Lamb wrote to her son about his lessons and how he would need them later 'if it please God you live'. But it was still heartbreaking. A father who lost two daughters in one year wrote to his brother: 'God bless you and your children, but do not love them.' Religious faith was of course a consolation, though perhaps not always a help. The second Viscount Halifax and his wife seem to have neglected some simple health measures which might have saved their three sons' lives, because of their readiness to accept that it was God's will that they should die. It is strange today to hear the poor father tell himself, when his first son died, that the boy would 'do more good for us where he is than he could have done in any other way.'

Parents were ready for their own deaths, and liked to say a proper goodbye to their children. In 1873, before giving birth to Lady Ottoline Morrell, her mother wrote a letter to her ten-year-old son. 'If God takes me from you this is to bid you farewell,' she wrote. 'I pray to God to comfort you, if I go, as I pray him to spare me to you if it is His will.' She then told the boy that God would take care of him if he asked Him to, and urged him always to read the Bible and say his prayers, 'for God loves them who love Him'. She hoped he would be 'persevering' in his studies, 'and try when you are older to do good in the world, to make a name worthy of your ancestors and of yourself'. Then she came down to more immediate matters. 'I think you will be happy in the schools we have chosen for you, Cheam and Eton, and that you will go to Oxford.' It was thoughtful of her to put these guidelines on paper for her son to keep. But, as it happened, she did not die.

Death brought especially big changes to the children of the aristocracy. Their parents' and their own names and titles might alter, they might suddenly find themselves much richer or poorer, or move to a different house in another part of the country – probably going from a relatively homely one to a palace with endless, huge, strange rooms which until then they had known only occasionally on visits to their grandparents. Sometimes death brought the children uncertainty and loss of status. Wilfred Scawen Blunt, the poet and traveller, was born at Petworth House, but when he was two his father died and the family moved to the rectory in the town. His Scottish Presbyterian nurse had taught him to abhor Roman Catholicism, and this must have been disturbing when his mother became a convert, and was followed soon afterwards by her children.

When a mother died, a grandmother, aunt or older sister usually took on the care of her children. The oldest Gurney daughter was sixteen when she inherited the mothering of her younger brothers and sisters, and she did it so well that she became known as 'Mrs Catherine Gurney'. A father's remarriage would bring a strange stepmother on the scene, perhaps with children of her own already, perhaps soon to present her husband with a second brood. It was not always an easy situation. A year after Robert Bowen's wife died, he married again. But the children refused to accept their stepmother. A cousin remembered them, 'black as crows and with their blue eyes starting out of their heads'. The second Mrs Bowen, perhaps because of the blue-eyed crows, survived only four years. There was a different complication when Frances Maynard's father and grandfather both died when she was three, and suddenly almost all the vast family inheritance became hers. Her mother took her two little girls to live at Easton Lodge, with its twelve hundred acres of parks, herds of deer and many farms and cottages. The rest of the family were so angry about the will that Frances's mother dared not let the children and their nurse ever go beyond the gardens without a strong manservant to guard them.

Death almost always took place in the home, and children were taken to say goodbye and to see the dead for the last time. There seems to have been no feeling that they should be spared these distressing moments. When the eighth Duke of Argyll was five and his brother was seven, their mother died and the little boys were taken to her room. He always remembered her urging them both to read the Scriptures every night and morning, and soon afterwards his father took him to see her in her coffin and to kiss her cold forehead. Sometimes the confrontation was even more dramatic. After the seventh Marquess of Queensberry was found shot in the grounds of his Scottish estate, his three-year-old twins were coming back from a drive with their nurse when they saw something heavy, covered by a cloak, being carried into the house. The family stood around in horrified silence. 'It's Papa, Papa's dead,' one twin explained to the other. 'The gun killed him like it kills a rabbit.' Then as now, death was not easy for small children to understand. Sacheverell Sitwell was two when his grandfather died, and he asked where he was. Away, he was told. It was not a good enough answer. 'Gone puff-puff?' he persisted. 'Gone ship?'

Even when children were not on the spot, a parent's death was dramatic. The fourth Marchioness of Salisbury was very young when her mother died, leaving four children under six. They were staying with relations at the time, and she had been ill and away so long that they really hardly knew her. But her daughter remembered the happenings of that day in detail all her life. The little girls were lunching downstairs when they were fetched to go up to the nursery – not, as usual, by their own nurse, but by their cousins', who was in tears. They found the nursery table piled with black cloth, from which their nurse was cutting frocks for them. One of the little girls said she would not dream of wearing a black frock – unless she was given a puzzle she had been longing for. Little did she know that there would be many more family deaths and that it would be years before they wore coloured frocks again. Lady Salisbury remembered being about seven when she wore her first pair of mauve, half-mourning stockings, and looked to see whether the policeman at the corner of Hertford Street had noticed them. Black crape was worn for relations and royals as well as for parents. After a close family death all the house and stable staff also wore deep black, and even a baby's clothes were sometimes trimmed with black rosettes.

All these funeral trappings, added to the fact that in many families they carried undertones of eternal torment and punishment, gave some children agonizing fears and nightmares. Many parents were sympathetic about these: one mother considerately cut the pages containing a poem about the death of the babes in the wood out of her little girl's book. And Sir George Sitwell proved very encouraging when Osbert told his father how terrified he was of hell. 'My dear boy', said Sir George, 'if you go to hell, you'll certainly find all the people you most admire there already – Wellington, Nelson and the Black Prince – and they'll discover a way of getting you out of it soon enough!'

6

Sickness and Health

Perhaps nothing has changed more since the nineteenth century than illness and health, and methods of treating them. Good health, strength and even youth were perishable blessings – to be thankful for, not taken for granted. Even happy occasions like christenings were overshadowed by anxiety, and so of course were weddings, with their promise – or was it a threat? – of endless childbearing. Most of the brides were very young, and many of them either died within a few years or were gradually transformed into frail invalids, condemned even in their thirties to lying languidly on a couch, without the vitality to enjoy the games and rompings of the children who filled the house.

The worst terrors were the infectious illnesses which swooped down on the whole population, threatening aristocratic families in their sheltered environment as well as the crowded inhabitants of industrial slums. Cholera was a dreaded scourge, and there was anxious talk of where it had turned up and what should be done. In London in 1854 people hung black warning flags over districts where it raged most fiercely, and most of the country house families felt safest away from town. But wives of Parliamentary husbands were in a quandary: they did not want the family separated in a time of danger, but the country was certainly safer than London. Some decided to join their husbands in town, leaving the children in faraway safety with their nurses.

Many treatments and medicines were hardly less frightening than the illnesses they were believed to cure. It is distressing now to see how often these must have been useless, if not actually harmful or even fatal. One nurse poured cans of cold water down the children's backs every morning to prevent them catching cold; a delicate baby was bathed in the sea in October; and the Sitwells were 'flayed alive' with strong mustard baths and doses of ipecacuanha, a South American shrub which acted as a purgative and made them sweat and vomit. A baby cutting his first tooth was given twenty drops of chloroform to inhale for ten minutes. The universally trusted panacea was what Byron's mother

72

called 'the perpetual leech' which, in partnership with the drawing-off of blood by 'cupping', must have got rid of quantities of valuable blood cells. 'Afflictions of the head' were treated by a succession of leeches, six at a time, one after the other on a child's scalp for as long as three days at a stretch. Five leeches were applied to the throat of a child who had scarlatina to 'bring out the infection'. Swollen glands, sprains and bruises, and dental abscesses were also treated with leeches. Even young babies did not escape them.

Illnesses which struck at children then but may need explaining now include ague, a feverish shivering fit; croup, an inflammation of the larynx and trachea which brought a painful hard cough and breathing difficulty; the thrush, a very sore mouth and throat condition; and the purples, a rash believed to be due to 'poorly' blood. They also had epilepsy, dysentery, erysipelas, diarrhoea and convulsions. Typhus, smallpox, diphtheria and scarlet fever were among illnesses which could prove fatal to either a young patient or his devoted nurse. One alarming account tells of a girl who developed scarlet fever while the ten children of the family were on holiday in a rented house at Brighton, with only two nursery staff to look after them. Treatment consisted of cutting off all the girl's hair so that 'cooling lotions' could be applied to her head; she was dosed with calomel and scaunory, and nourished with a teaspoon of wine in some gruel, followed by a teaspoon of brandy with two drops of laudanum. She managed to survive both illness and treatment, though the doctor insisted that she must not attempt any 'brain-work' for two months.

Quite a lot of children suffered from nervous strain and terrors of various kinds. From an early age Byron was terrified at night, used to search his room carefully, ordered his servant to check that no one was lurking under the bed, and at one time had a ladder and ropes at the ready in case the house caught fire. Osbert Sitwell, when he was about ten, slept in a room at Renishaw where he heard strange sounds, and every night he dreamed that his grandfather, who had been dead forty years, sat by him and talked to him.

Gradually some modern medical ideas – such as the use of chloroform in childbirth and vaccination against smallpox – came to be accepted by a few pioneers. But even the intelligentsia of the day had some odd practices, or at least allowed these in the people they employed to look after their children. Rosalind, the celebrated Countess of Carlisle whose political and social outlook was well ahead of her times, believed in 'heart baths' for her children, took them to 'cures' in England and on the Continent, and at one time insisted that they, their tutor and she herself should go about barefoot, out-of-doors as well as indoors, through most of a cold snowy winter. The Gladstone children had good health – though two letters mention that they had flea-bites – but Catherine Gladstone could not breast-feed her second baby. Asses' milk was prescribed for her, so a donkey went along with them when the parents travelled. One nurse was convinced that fresh air was bad for children inside the house, and she gave them any left-over medicines indiscriminately because she did not want to waste them and hoped that they would 'scare away' any illnesses that might be on the way. But it was not only ignorant nurses who did such things. Countess Gower wrote in 1832 that her children were well, but she was about to dose them *par précaution* before a five-day journey.

Among the silliest and most painful treatments inflicted on children were those which aimed at producing beauty or a dignified deportment in young girls. Many of them had to have a rest after lunch on hard wood, to encourage a straight back and neck. The future Duchess of Westminster was made by her mother to wear a mahogany backboard which was strapped round her arms and then tightened and buckled at the back. Even worse, she had a violin string fastened tightly round her shoulders so that it cut sharply into her arms whenever she leaned forward. She had to wear it all day, even for games, and when the violin string snapped she had to buy another with her own pocket-money. Of course Edith Sitwell's parents managed to think up an even crueller torture. While she was still in the schoolroom they noticed that she stooped slightly and so took her to an orthopaedic surgeon in London. He prescribed that she should be 'imprisoned in steel which began under my arms, preventing me from resting them on my sides'. Her legs were clamped in metal down to her ankles, and when she went to bed her ankles and the soles of her feet were 'locked in an excruciating contraption'. The Sitwell parents did not like the shape of their daughter's nose, so at night she had to wear a piece of steel on each side of it suspended from an elastic band round her forehead. Thick pads on her nostrils were intended to turn her nose the opposite way to that intended by nature, but in fact all they did was block one nostril and make it difficult for her to breathe.

At Knole, Vita Sackville-West's grandfather used to squirt the juice of orange peel into her eyes. When she screamed at the pain he reminded her of the Spanish gypsy dancer who had been her grandmother and explained that Spanish mothers did this to make their daughters' eyes beautiful. It was not much better at Inveraray in Scotland, where the very short-sighted daughter of the Duke of Argyll was not given spectacles because these were considered unbecoming. For years she had to manage with only a toy telescope to help her, and it was Princess Louise – the Queen's daughter who taught her how to sew on buttons – who transformed her life by giving her her first pair of spectacles.

After such ordeals it is a relief to turn back to the milder treatments that children were given. Among these were blue pills, black doses and various evil-sounding powders – James's, Gregory, rhubarb and liquorice, among others. A 'change of air' was sometimes advised, and it might have been expected that in those splendid homes plenty of good wholesome food would help to keep the children well and strong. Sometimes it did, but many parents and nurses had odd theories which often sent the younger generation hungry to bed. At Inveraray, again, the Duke's children were said to be 'always hungry'. Their main meal was luncheon with their parents, and there were so many at the table that by the time the youngest child was given his helping, their grandfather had finished eating. He then rose, and the meal was over. They never had anything sweet as it was believed to be bad for them. Of course this made them long for sugar, so they used to raid the dishes that were carried out of the dining-room during the evening meal.

Old Earl Russell and his wife also reared their grandson on a spartan diet. They held that sugar and fruit were bad for children, and they filled the gaps in his menu with various carbohydrates. An old French lady who was a friend of theirs used to give him boxes of delicious chocolates, but his grandparents rationed these strictly. He was allowed one every Sunday but on weekdays had to hand them round for the grown-ups to help themselves. As for fruit, at luncheon an orange was served to everyone at the table – except for him. He wondered later why he was never ill, and decided that he was probably saved by stealing crab-apples. The ban on fruit led him to tell his first lie when his governess asked whether he had been eating blackberries. No, he answered; but his blue-black tongue gave the game away.

At Renishaw the young Sitwells were reared on boiled mutton, a 'stodgy eternity of rice pudding' and a 'pale eternity of jelly'. Osbert managed to purloin sultanas and candied cherries from the sympathetic kitchen staff. The children's nurse, 'dear old Davis', considered bananas to be 'common' and that winkles and shrimps were also not fit food for ladies and gentlemen. But children were children, she allowed, and when they were at Scarborough she could not resist buying them. When Osbert had the croup, both Davis and the doctor thwarted his instinctive longing for oranges, which he always felt would have cured him, so back he went to sago pudding, blancmange and calves' foot jelly.

One or two of the great families were faced with the personal tragedy of a physically or mentally handicapped child. In 1827 the eldest son of the second Marquess of Salisbury was born slightly prematurely and was a delicate, undersized baby. They soon noticed that though he was intelligent, his sight was weak and he was getting more and more deaf. His parents did everything possible for him, sending him to a consultant in Berlin and on cruises in the Mediterranean and Adriatic with a tutor who was also a doctor. Gradually they came to accept that the boy would never have normal health, sight or hearing, and Lord Salisbury took him to Devonshire to be looked after and taught by a clergyman there. It is not clear why they sent him so far from home, but he showed himself to be cheerful and able, especially interested in history, and his essays and books on the French Revolution are still at Hatfield. Of course it was particularly distressing that this disaster had occurred to Lord Salisbury's heir. In 1865 he died, and his brother Robert, the future Prime Minister, succeeded him as Viscount Cranborne.

Lord Melbourne, one of the Queen's earlier Prime Ministers, also had a seriously handicapped son. As soon as he was born, in 1807, Augustus Lamb's 'odd helpless countenance' was unmistakable to everyone except Lady Caroline, his over-fond mother. She was herself mentally unstable and when she was ten had been so highly strung that a doctor had been sent for. He had ordered that she must be allowed to do whatever she liked, and she was in fact alternately indulged and neglected. After Augustus was born she had recurring fits of insanity, often brought on by drink or laudanum, and she used to dress up and go out alone in odd clothes. In fact if Augustus's 'vacant look' had not been so noticeable from the first, it might have seemed that his mother's behaviour had affected him. Caroline's cousin told how she 'rides out upon the high road, the Horse or Ass. . .led by a page in full dress, the baby on her lap and her maid and the nurses following on foot and then wonders why the Turnpike men laugh at her'.

But poor Augustus was much worse. Teething threw him into convulsions and at three he had violent fits of temper. When he was five he

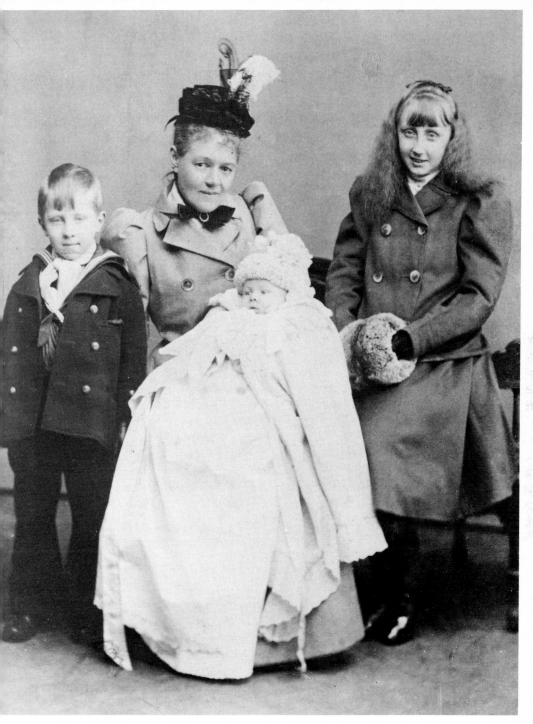

'Dear old Davis . . . with her usual expression of kind and puzzled patience' has Sacheverell Sitwell on her lap and Osbert and Edith on either side.

could hardly speak intelligibly, and his mental age was never more than that of a child of eight. But he was tall and muscular, quite capable of rushing undressed into a room, throwing a maid or his old nurse on the floor and sitting on her. He pinched the maids, terrifying them by jumping on them, hurt the dogs and hit one of the women with a cricket-ball. His parents were baffled, and their treatment of him reflects the inconsistency of their attitudes. Sometimes they called in a succession of doctors; sometimes they refused to recognize his abnormality and engaged a tutor to teach philosophy to a boy who found the three R's beyond him. They tried giving him less to eat than he wanted; they brought out the inevitable leeches, 'magnetized' him daily, applied 'metallic tractors' to draw away 'the obnoxious fluids', and at least once they scorched his skull with caustic acid. But there was little if any improvement, though Augustus was lovable and his parents, relations and the servants all gave him plenty of affection. Susan Churchill, Caroline's illegitimate cousin whom the Lambs adopted and brought up, was specially close to him. She was eleven years younger, so they could play happily together.

Less serious handicaps also left their mark on children. Byron was always aware of his malformed foot and was anxious to be reassured that his daughter had not inherited the abnormality. In spite of his dislike of his mother, his attitude to his lameness must have been influenced by hers. She took his disability, together with his striking good looks and his powerful athletic body, as a sign that he was fated to be a great man. Nevertheless she did what she could and sent him to Nottingham, where his leg was screwed into a painful wooden frame. It did not help much, but probably caused less lasting damage than a remark made by his beautiful cousin, Mary Chaworth, one of Byron's childhood loves. 'Do you think', he heard her say to her maid, 'I could care anything for that lame boy?' Her words pierced him, he said later, like 'a shot through the heart'.

The presence of illness or madness in the house has its effect, of course, on children, and in the great families – as in humbler ones – there was plenty of both. Memoirs, letters and diaries mention invalid or deranged grandparents, sisters, brothers and cousins. Some had been in institutions for years; but the great houses were usually sufficiently large and well staffed for them to be cared for at home. Lord Berners tells of his lunatic grandfather who lived with them and took part, sometimes rather strangely, in their family life. When the old man's behaviour was particularly odd the children were told that he was 'bewitched'. Another grandparent who suffered from what they called 'nervous illness and depression' was old Lady Glynne. She lived at Hagley, the home of her Lyttelton grandchildren, in her own set of rooms. The children were told not to go up the stairs near her sitting-room, and were made to keep quiet on her side of the house. As she grew older and stranger they gradually left off going to visit her, regarding her, as one of them later put it, 'more as a sort of awful mystery than anything else'.

There were other cases of devotedly affectionate care of mental invalids. The fifteenth Duke of Norfolk spent every possible moment alone with his blind, deaf and dumb son, who had the mental age of a new-born baby. And at Petworth, not far away, one of Lord Leconfield's four daughters was capable of little beyond gentle walks and simple needlework. But her father, after his wife died, lived on in the great house with her in a deeply affectionate relationship.

The doctors of the day were a varied bunch. Until 1815 the law allowed medicines to be prescribed and dispensed by apothecaries with no formal medical training. George Russell has left a splendid description of the doctors of the second half of the nineteenth century, as they appeared to the children they treated. He remembered them 'always dressed in shiny black – trousers, neckcloth, and all; they were invariably bald, and had shaved upper lips and chins, and carefully trimmed whiskers. They said 'Hah!' and 'Hum!' in tones of omniscience which would have converted a Christian Scientist; and, when feeling one's pulse, they produced the largest and most audibly-ticking gold watches conceivable.' He went on to say that they never spoke of the stomach, always of 'the gastric organ'; never said brandy, always 'the domestic stimulant'. But Russell seems to have approved of their prescriptions. He was a delicate boy, and the doctors said he should have a glass of port at eleven o'clock, often with a teaspoonful of 'bark', as quinine was then called. If he showed signs of weakness, brandy-and-water was the order of the day, and if this did not mend matters, more brandy was to be added. When he was twelve, Russell was prescribed mulled claret at bedtime, and he was happy to report that he found that a far better nightcap than bromide and sulphonal.

7

Rank and Class

The children of the great country houses grew up cocooned in class-consciousness. Only the most questioning of the Hons and rebels challenged the rightness of the social *status quo*. The families were insulated from contact with other classes by the houses themselves and the rolling acres of parkland that surrounded them. The only 'others' they were likely to meet were servants, tenants, villagers and – in the case of families who were given to good works – the deserving poor, and all of these were of course conditioned to accept the system. One devout viscount voiced his conviction that 'Almighty God had placed people in certain stations of life and clearly intended them to remain in them'. It was a comfortable line for the rich man in his castle to take, and curiously enough it was probably reassuring also for the poor man at his gate. That is how it must have looked, and it is not easy to imagine what arguments might have been found to make the viscount think differently. Yet he was a father who was happy for his sons to spend their time playing cricket with the village boys and to go ratting and ferreting with the keepers.

So the first view of the outside world from the nursery window was of gardens well kept, lawns well mown and parkland well ordered by cap-touching employees. Visits to other houses must have given the impression that elsewhere it was on roughly the same lines that life went on. The children's place in the pattern was well defined. Lord Longford remembers going with his brothers, sisters and cousins when they were young to the splendid parties given by his grandmother, the Dowager Countess of Jersey, at Osterley. They were great social occasions, and the children took them in their stride. One of his grandmother's guests asked the young Pakenhams who they were. 'We are the grandchildren of grandpapa!' young Frank answered, and no more needed to be said. One child who did not learn till she was grown-up that she was not in fact the grandchild of her grandpapa and that her father was not, as she had always thought, the Duke of Rutland, nevertheless had the social hierarchy imprinted on her at an early age. Lady Diana Cooper used to be taken, wrapped in an eiderdown, from her night-nursery to see her beautiful mother in sparkling jewels and splendid dress as she went off to the great dinners and balls of the time.

Children who forgot the exalted social group they belonged to had plenty of people at the ready to remind them. It would be good to have a tape-recording of conversation in those nurseries and schoolrooms, as there are too few accounts of how nurses, governesses and their charges used to speak to each other. One lively dialogue described by Byron's daughter, the Countess of Lovelace, shows a nurse addressing a little boy as 'My Lord' as well as by his Christian name. Young Byron, as they called him, did not like his nurse, Mrs Norton, and interrupted her chatter by saying that he would like the horses to kick her. 'Oh my Lord,' the nurse protested, 'now that's very ill-natured and unkind to Mrs Norton; oh Fie! And Mrs Norton is so very kind to Byron too. I'm sure you wouldn't like Mrs Norton to be hurt, – would you now?' '*Like it*', Byron insisted, and his mother's account adds that his mind was quite made up that she was an old chatterbox and he 'wished her at the Deuce, if he had but known how to express it'.

Vita Sackville-West's governess was one of those who liked to encourage decorous behaviour in her charge by a reminder of the ancient family she belonged to. 'My child, remember who you *are*', she used to say; and when she was older a similar – but no doubt equally ineffective – appeal was made: 'Oh my dears, do consider your illus-trious names.' But then Vita, who loved getting muddy and dirty in games with the farm children, was hardly a governess's dream child. On holiday in Scotland she ran wild over the hills, walked for miles with the guns, spent whole days fishing on the loch, and was just like the farmers' children she played with. One local boy was a year older and wiser than she was and, she remembered, told her many things he should not have done. Even so, at that time she was very snobbish – in an original way. She felt that aristocrats and working people had a lot in common, but she despised the middle classes that came between them. The Sackville family language had a contemptuous, much-used word for these: they called them 'bedints'.

Social divisiveness was reinforced by the private schools that aristocratic parents chose carefully for their sons and for the few daughters who, at a later age, were sent to London day-schools. At some schools the sons of peers sat on a separate bench, away from the other boys; and when the Duke of Argyll's grandsons went to Eton they lived in a special house there, with their own tutor. But during the nineteenth century parents noticed that schools were being ominously infiltrated by a class of moneyed newcomers. This eventually gave the social mix an invigorating shake-up, but it took a long time. Even during the first years of this century Lady Blanche Cobbold had no social contact at Chatsworth, she recently recalled, with contemporaries outside her own class. Surely her brothers brought a wider cross-section of Eton friends to stay with them during the holidays? No, she answered; it was mostly cousins who came to stay, and the girls never saw any young people from a different *milieu*. No doubt this was the result of a deliberate policy, conscious or not, whose end-result was the narrowing of the field of choice for future husbands. Sons, of course, inevitably got out into the wider world and so could not altogether be prevented from making *mésalliances*.

One possible means of broadening the children's social range were the classes for special subjects like art and dancing that were attended by some of those who were educated at home. There they were likely to meet local children from less aristocratic homes, which is probably why grandparents tended to disapprove of them. At least one of these took care to give a different reason for her objection. In 1843 Lady Stanley told her daughter-in-law that she thought she 'half-killed' her children with her 'novelty education mania'; the drawing-class that her grand-daughter, 'poor, unfortunate, delicate, ailing Blanche' went to was specially condemned for being crowded and hot. Blanche seems to have been going for strenuous long rides on her pony at that time, but none-theless Lady Stanley's advice was taken and a drawing-master was engaged to come to the house.

Sometimes it was the other children, not those from the big house, who won the day. The young Wyndhams from Petworth House tried throwing the weight of their family inheritance around. '*My* father has a fire-engine!' they boasted, which did not endear themselves to the other children at their local dancing-class. They must have been set apart already, but the fact that their father was the owner not only of the house, park and most of the surrounding town and land, but also of the splendid horse-drawn fire-engine, with its brass boiler and 'Lord Leconfield' painted in large capital letters on it, certainly did nothing to bridge the gap. The Sitwell children absorbed a similar pride of birth when the Earl of Londesborough took them and his other grandchildren

Mrs Stanley, later Lady Stanley of Alderley, in 1811, with her sons Edward and William.
The boys were twins, born in 1802, but are still wearing girlish clothes.

to the circus at Scarborough where a quarter of the seats were reserved for the family, and to the town's great Cricket Week where once again he ruled the roost.

Such great occasions gave children a sense of their own and their family's dignity, though sometimes this had to be reinforced by further coaching in social solidarity. When Lady Gregory was a child in Ireland she heard Irish spoken every day and asked to be taught it. No, she was told; Irish was a language for servants and peasants, not for ladies. So she had to wait till her son had the same wish, and the two of them taught themselves from an Irish grammar and an old Irish Bible they borrowed. A similar lesson was given to Blanche Balfour at Inveraray when she was eight. One day she had been arguing with her aunt outside the door of the church, and was told that she had broken 'the law about dignity and reticence in the presence of "people of a different class"'. The lessons must often have borne fruit, as can be seen from a description of Lord Dalmeny when he was thirteen. 'His patrician *hauteur* was unmistakable', one of his Eton contemporaries wrote. 'Not an offensive *hauteur*, but that calm pride by which a man seems to ascend in a balloon out of earshot every time he is addressed by one not socially his equal.' Beaks even more than boys must have borne the brunt of that *hauteur*.

Often it was schoolmasters and others 'not socially equal' who were the first to kowtow to a title. Byron was ten when he inherited the barony of Newstead. He was sent for by his headmaster, who gave him some cake and wine and told him that his great-uncle had died. Byron remembered later that the treat and the master's respectful manner gave him 'high notions of his own dignity' at once, though in fact the main difference his succeeding to the title brought him was that he was made a ward in Chancery. Often it did bring big changes which reverberated round the various branches of the family and had probably been expected for years. The thirteenth Duke of Bedford must surely be unique in knowing nothing of his 'prospects' until he was sixteen. He had an isolated childhood, never went to school, and did not know that he was related to the previous Duke – let alone that he was his heir – until one of the maids told him. Hardly less puzzling was Edith Sitwell's experience when her mother, in some of her frequent rages at her daughter, clinched matters by her final claim: '*I* am better-born than *you* are.' Her grounds were that she was an earl's daughter, whereas Edith's father (her own husband) was only a baronet. As it happened, when the Earl eventually died there were legal complications and the Sitwells for a time at least felt themselves confronted by poverty. The main effect of this on the children was that their presents now had to be 'useful' things like soap, toothbrushes and shoelaces. Edith was of course already used to coming last in her family's esteem. An old lady who was a close family friend gave both her brothers a gold sovereign four times a year, but because she was a girl there was never one for Edith.

Distance lends enchantment to the view, and no doubt that was why working people had a certain glamour in some children's eyes. William Lamb, the future Lord Melbourne, used to sit at his desk at school, watching the labourers at work outside in the grounds, and longing to be one of them. Byron's five-year-old grandson shared those feelings, and backed them up with some good arguments and eventually with actions. His mother described how young Byron 'has the utmost aversion to the term *Gentleman*; & says that a *gentleman* is a *smart man*: & that for his part, he wishes to be like Wheel Ridler (one of the workmen here) & never a *smart man*. He seems not to have the remotest conception of *rank*; or of any dignities attached to *titles* of any sort.' It was early to take such an independent stand, and Byron kept to it, braving the disapproval of his father and grandmother by ignoring his rank and doing the workmen's jobs alongside them. His grandmother complained of the children's '*rude vulgar* tone of language' and 'coarse servant-like way of talking', and was told by the governess that Byron had caught this from the workmen and that his sister copied him.

At Castle Howard both parents and children had democratic, egalitarian principles. The Howards sent the head cook off to her wedding from the castle, and all took part in the service and celebrations. The story went round that Cecilia Howard had a hundred and seventy-eight bridesmaids when she married, but in fact they were her two youngest sisters and the senior girls from the schools on the estate, all of whom she had taught in Sunday School, so they knew each other well. The tenants and locals referred to the Earl of Carlisle somewhat quaintly as 'the Lord', but many of the older ones, who had known him as a boy, called him George. Even at Castle Howard, however, democratic ideas had their limits, and there was never much chance of Oliver fulfilling his ambition to be a jockey, though he starved himself and took clandestine tots of gin to 'keep short'. Noble birth nipped other aspirations in the bud. Edward Stanley eventually became a revered bishop, but as a boy he dreamed only of the sea and longed to become a sailor. Once when he was missing from his cot he was found, fast asleep, high up on a wardrobe shelf where he had climbed because he thought it was like a ship's berth.

There were other ways that the upper and working classes met – or thought they met. Osbert Sitwell said that he 'never experienced the sensation of being separate from the working classes in the way that city-bred, middle-class poets and the proletarian movement continually proclaim to feel themselves cut off'. The reason for this, he suggested, was that he came of a family which had lived within the same three miles for at least seven hundred years, so that they and the neighbouring work-people had drawn their strength from the same soil. The Sitwell children certainly had vigorous contacts with working people – Henry Moat, their father's idiosyncratic butler; his brother, who was a fisherman; various gardeners; the aged and devout Mary Anne, who looked after the birds on the lake, living in a cottage on the island there, and later inspiring a poem of Osbert's; and the skipper of the local lifeboat, a great friend whom they often visited, and who initiated them into the mysteries of his boat. Probably the closest contact of all was when Osbert, aged three, got his own way in the face of parental opposition and went with his nurse, Davis, to visit her father, a cobbler in a little Berkshire village. All his life he remembered the unfamiliar enchantment of waking up in the small cottage room, of sitting in the old man's workshop, watching him as he hammered away at his last, listening to him as he talked to his friends, and playing with Davis's many nieces and nephews.

Most families had a warm, if somewhat paternalistic, contact with their less fortunate neighbours through their acceptance of the responsibilities that are now borne by professional social workers. Children took an active part in all this. George Russell describes the closeness of these links at Woburn. Once again there was the feeling that through the long centuries all had been nourished by the same soil, the awareness that faces, homes and family histories were known to everyone. The children from the big house were sent out to visit cottages where there was illness or other troubles. Among the first lessons they learned were the basic *politesses* of always knocking before opening a door, waiting to be asked before sitting down, and taking care not to turn up when a family was likely to be having a meal. The Russell boys got to know the village on the cricket pitch, and at the parish church they were confirmed alongside farmers' and keepers' sons, and flirted with the vicar's daughter while they decorated the lectern with

Christmas holly. The girls were at home more than their brothers, and so had a more lasting contact. They played with the babies in the cottages and farms, taught the children when they were old enough to go to Sunday School, delivered meals – on horse-drawn wheels at that time – to those who needed them, read cheering or pious passages beside sickbeds, and finally brought bunches of flowers to lay on coffins.

8

Bastards and Break-ups

Warm nests of affection, respectability and regular church-going though they often were, many of the great nineteenth-century dynasties were blessed with one or more bastard children as well as their legitimate brood. The conventions of the day allowed these to be born to married women who slipped discreetly away to the Continent before their silhouettes began to attract attention. Their babies were born abroad, and a few months later back they came to their homes and husbands. Some of the children were brought back and welcomed into their mother's nursery, to be loved, cared for and accepted alongside their legitimate half-siblings; some were looked after by faithful retainers, kindly grandparents or other relatives. The unlucky ones landed up in the Foundling Hospital – a fate which may, without Nelson's knowledge, have been that of Horatia's twin, born to him by Emma Hamilton.

Between the two extremes of affectionate acceptance and chilly cold-shouldering there were various intermediate ups-and-downs. Bastard children were not usually given their father's surname, though he might well provide property or funds for them. One of the happiest and most flexible set-ups was that of the fifth Duke of Devonshire in the years just before the nineteenth century began. His first illegitimate child was Charlotte, the result of an affair he had in his twenties with a parson's daughter whom he later discreetly set up as a milliner. The child was given the surname of Williams, and it was arranged that a Mrs Garner should look after her. The Duke's marriage to Lady Georgiana Spencer was a strange one, and for the first eight years there were no children. At last the Duchess gave birth to a daughter, mainly because the tactful presence in the household of the Duke's mistress, Lady Elizabeth Foster – who was also the Duchess's 'dearest friend' –had the effect of bringing the couple more closely together in every sense. Eventually Mrs Garner's services were dispensed with, and Charlotte was sent off to a fashionable school in London.

The *ménage à trois* jogged on, and both the Duchess and Lady Elizabeth bore the Duke a daughter within a month of each other. Lady Elizabeth was welcomed into the Devonshire household with her baby, and both the Duke and the Duchess were devoted to her though cold to each other. The children, bastard and legitimate alike, grew up and played together in the well-feathered Cavendish nest. For years the Duke waited in vain for an heir; the son he had by Lady Elizabeth was born in Normandy and left with a foster-mother there. Even when the Duchess did at last give birth to a boy, the Duke had more love for the illegitimate children he knew less well than for those who had been born to his wife. It is interesting to see that when, a year after the birth of the Duke's heir, the Duchess became pregnant by Charles Grey, there was no question of her bastard being welcomed into the Devonshire nursery as her husband's had been. The baby was adopted and brought up by her grandfather, Earl Grey. Yet the Duke had hoped to persuade John Foster, Lady Elizabeth's husband, to allow her two legitimate sons to join the Devonshire house family. Foster refused, and it was not till their father's death when the boys were in their late teens that they all came together and the Duke paid for both boys to go to Oxford.

So even with tolerance and goodwill, things were not altogether straightforward. Caroline St Jules, Lady Elizabeth's daughter by the Duke, was not told who her father was till she was about to be married. It seems strange that it was then her husband-to-be who told her, and that the Duke settled the same fortune on Caroline as he did on his elder legitimate daughter when she married the Earl of Carlisle's heir. No doubt the illegitimate children in the Devonshire House set felt secure and that they 'belonged' just because there were so many of them. Known as the 'Children of the Mist', they grew up in a genealogical tangle which was made even more complex by their subsequent marriages. William Lamb, Lord Melbourne, who is believed to have been the illegitimate son of Lord Egremont, put the matter in a nutshell. 'Who the devil can tell who's anybody's father?' he asked. A good question. . .

It was a very different matter when a child was born to an unmarried mother. Complete secrecy was then the order of the day, and the families concerned, however noble, often pretended they knew nothing about it. There was an unusual case when in 1818 Lady Harriet Spencer, an unmarried cousin of the Duke of Devonshire, gave birth to a daughter, Susan Churchill, after being seduced by the Marquess of Blandford. The Spencers ignored the child's existence so Lady Bessborough, another cousin, stood godmother to her and gave her a home till her death four years later. After that, Lady Bessborough's daughter Caroline and her husband William Lamb took her into their family, treating her as a younger sister to their retarded son, Augustus, giving her a happy – if somewhat irregular – childhood and as good an education as a girl could then have. Susan was unlike the illegitimate children of married women of her class in that she was born in London and was given her father's surname. Nevertheless until she married she was not told who her father was, and in her marriage settlement she was referred to as an orphan.

William and Caroline Lamb gave Susan plenty of affection and she returned it devotedly, naming her own first two children after her adoptive parents. There are very few hints that she was in any way disadvantaged – just the occasional reference to 'poor Susan' and, when she was about eight, a letter to Augustus telling him of 'your little wife Susan', who 'is doing her sums as she means to be your housekeeper by and by'. That, of course, was the question: what would become of her when she grew up? Susan in fact found a good husband in Switzerland, but otherwise the monstrous regiment of governesses might well have been the only future open to her.

The stigma of illegitimacy was sometimes harder to bear and could leave a deep scar. The third Earl of Egremont had six illegitimate children by a mistress whom he 'kept upstairs' for years at Petworth before at long last he married her. George Wyndham, the eldest of their children, was tormented all his life by shame at his illegitimacy, which made him isolate himself and his family from the village a few yards from his walls, forbidding his children to have any contact with the towns-people. In other families it was the relatives who ostracised the bastard children. After the death of the Spanish dancer he had loved and lived with for years, Lionel Sackville-West brought their four children to England, where they met with a mixed reception. They were bewildered to find that one of their uncles was an earl and the owner of a great country house called Buckhurst, that another was Lord Sackville who owned Knole, and that both the Duchess of Bedford and the Countess of Derby were their aunts. Lady Bedford refused to open her park gates to her embarrassing relatives, but Lady Derby was kindness itself, welcoming them to Derby House – on occasions when no visitors were present.

Marriage break-ups, then as now, often harmed children more than doubts about their legitimacy. There was never much chance of Lord Byron's marriage surviving for long and in 1815, soon after his daughter was born, off he went. Ada grew up with a mother who lived in continual terror that Byron might claim custody of the child, and that he might even have a shot at kidnapping her. Lady Byron was not the woman to resist a chance of dramatizing her situation, and when she and Ada visited her relations and friends she took with her two or more menservants to protect her daughter against a possible snatch by Byron's agents – though this never happened.

Fathers were considered at that time to be all-important in the begetting of children, so the law allowed them an almost absolute right to decide what should happen to them. If Byron, after leaving his wife, had offered to have her back with him, Lady Byron would have risked losing her custody of Ada. Byron never made that move, in spite of his passionate fondness for his only legitimate child and his grief at their lack of contact. When he first saw Ada, soon after she was born, he already foresaw this. 'Oh! what an implement of torture have I acquired in you!' were strange words to address to a new-born baby. Eight years later he was tormented by the thought that he knew nothing about his daughter. A letter to his half-sister, Augusta, begged her to get from Lady Byron:

> some account of Ada's disposition, habits, studies, moral tendencies, and temper, as well as her personal appearance, for except for the miniature drawn five years ago (and she is now nearly double that age) I have no idea of even her aspect... Is the girl imaginative... Is she social or solitary, taciturn or talkative, fond of reading or other-wise, and what is her *tic*? – I mean her foible – is she passionate? I hope that the Gods have made her anything save *poetical* – it is enough to have one such fool in the family.

Byron received the answers to his questions at Missolonghi, two months before he died.

What could Ada's feelings have been for her missing father? She was an exceptionally bright child and must have asked some direct questions. But just as Byron needed reassuring that Ada had not inherited his lameness, so Lady Byron was determined to ward off from Ada what she saw as the evil in her father's nature. She had odd ways of doing this. She hung a large portrait of Byron over a chimney-piece in her family home, but covered it with a curtain and insisted that Ada should not see the picture until she was twenty-one. It was not till long after Byron's death that Ada was allowed to see his handwriting. What danger of contamination could that have had? When the child's questions became insistent, she was fobbed off by being told that her father was a famous poet. Lady Byron was torn between pride in her marriage to such a romantic character and her desire to cut him down to size in his daughter's eyes.

When there was a tussle over the custody of children it was nearly always the mother who got the worst of it. A divorced woman, whether innocent or guilty, was banished from society. In 1836, the year before Queen Victoria's accession, a bush-fire of a scandal blazed up about Caroline Norton and Lord Melbourne, the Prime Minister, already in his late fifties but still very attractive to women. George Norton filed a petition against Lord Melbourne and sent his children to stay with relations, away from their mother's company and influence. Caroline was devoted to her children and became frantic when she heard that the Nortons were not treating them kindly. She drove down to the country where they were, and they threw themselves into her arms. But the family saw her as a danger and an enemy, wrenched them apart and turned poor Caroline out of the house. Eventually George Norton's case was heard, and it was decided that his charge was unfounded. But even so, Caroline was not allowed to have her children back.

So there was every reason for a society woman who had children to avoid the cataclysm of divorce, no matter how unhappily married she might be or how deeply in love with another man. The celebrated Countess of Warwick came very near to divorce within five years of her marriage. She was a woman of enough character and courage to face the hullabaloo, the disgrace and the loss of her children. But the crisis passed, leaving her soon to face an even greater scandal – though this time with no risk of divorce – when she became the mistress of the Prince of Wales, who was then nearing fifty and the father of five children.

Strangely enough, another desperate fight for the custody of a child as a result of a divorce also involved one of Lord Melbourne's women friends. This time the parents were Lord and Lady Brandon and the child was their daughter Lilly. The letters about the effect on the child of a parental split show a serious concern that she 'should be fretted as little as possible', and Lady Brandon's mother was among those who were dismayed at the possibility of mother and child being separated.

Lord Byron as a boy, a portrait by Sir Thomas Lawrence. 'I can, I will cut myself a path through the world or perish in the attempt', he resolved.

The old lady would, she declared, 'pack up and start for London and take Miss Lilly' rather than allow this to happen.

Two other parents who caused great neglect and unhappiness to their children by their broken marriage were the novelist Edward Bulwer-Lytton (he was created Baron Lytton in 1866) and his wife Rosina. When their son and daughter were nine and five the parents decided to separate on grounds of temperamental incompatibility, and the family home broke up. Rosina seems to have had no maternal feelings at all, so the children were taken care of by a friend of hers, a Miss Greene. She made a new home for them, tried to be both mother and father to them, gave them all she had – it was not much, either financially or intellectually – and dedicated her whole life to their care. Most of their childhood was spent with Miss Greene in a humble lodging-house in Cheltenham. They had hardly any toys or books, and not always enough to eat.

At this time, while his children were with Miss Greene, their father used to visit them for a week or so every year. It seems that the children never felt that he might have spared them a little more of his time. The boy, Teddy, who was to be Earl of Lytton and both Viceroy and Governor-General of India, adored his father, seeing him as a hero, brilliant, rich and beautiful. On one visit he brought with him his friend the writer, John Forster, and it was from him that Teddy received the encouragement and tenderness he needed. He was sent to school when he was eight, and spent his holidays either at school or with a tutor. Visits to John Forster's rooms in Lincoln's Inn Fields were red-letter occasions. Teddy often turned up in worn-out shoes and without enough clothes to keep the weather out, and kind John Forster bought these for him. He knew that Teddy loved the theatre and he took him to see Macready act, to dine with him in his rooms, and to visit his friend Charles Dickens.

9

Us and Them

How did the aristocratic children inside their turreted homes and behind their park railings ever get an inkling of the seamier side of life, of how the other half lived? In different ways and to different extents most of them did have some contact – often a close and active one – with Everyman. The most direct link was the feudal one between landlord and tenant, between the family up at the big house and the farmers and cottagers on the estate and in the village. There were also the 'good works' which the families undertook, enlisting their children to help them both because they were useful and because they considered it an important part of their upbringing. Although news and pictures of happenings at home and abroad were not repeatedly pumped into households at that time, even then there were newspapers, and reports arrived of election results, Crimean battles, cholera epidemics and industrial unrest. The company and conversation of servants were two other important lifelines which gave the children knowledge of working people's lives, and this was reinforced by what they came across as they walked or drove about town and country. They would notice ragged, hungry-looking beggars and tramps in the lanes, slums in the towns, and some of them faced up to the disquieting questions such glimpses posed. There are always others, of course, who never ask such questions, who never look over the social wall.

The children's contacts with tenants and neighbours have already been described. Often they bridged the gap effectively between the two worlds and the different generations; but some business errands the children were sent on were beyond them. In Ireland Robert Bowen's eldest daughter was only seventeen when she was sent to collect the rent from her father's farm tenants. Those were hard times, and she met some glum faces and stubborn refusals. How could she possibly press them for payment? She drove home chilled by the cold and 'crying with fear'. It could not have been hard to guess what her parents' reactions would be. Her father stubbornly insisted on his dues; but his wife often came to the rescue by quietly slipping the rent-money into empty hands.

The Gurney family must be included here because of the outstanding part so many of them played in the Quaker and philanthropical life of the early nineteenth century. Although they were not noble or titled, they lived in a great country house – though they only rented it – and were certainly upper-class. When they moved in to Earlham, outside Norwich, there were eight children; three more were born soon afterwards, and then their mother died. At sixteen Catherine took over the mothering of her large family with Rachel, who was fourteen, and Betsy, a year younger, to help her. And it was not just a matter of mothering. The sisters had themselves been reared in Quaker benevolence, and they set to work to pass this on to the younger children. Before he was two, Joseph was refusing to eat sugar because he had heard from his sister about the slaves who worked on the plantations. As a baby he had been nursed by the gardener's wife, who lived in a modest cottage inside the Earlham grounds. Joseph remained devoted to Nurse Norman, and when he was four or five he used to run off to share their family meal of apple dumplings with her and her children. His sister Betsy (Elizabeth Fry) was walking in the park one day when she met and started talking to a girl of about her own age. After hearing her story, Betsy spoke to her father and he agreed to adopt the girl. Soon after this Betsy began gathering children from nearby villages at Earlham, where she taught them. Before long there were seventy of them and they came to be known as 'Betsy's Imps'. She started a Sunday school in a room at the top of the house, and followed this with a small day-school for six girls in Norwich. She was as independent as she was enterprising, and became a 'plain' Quaker, which involved a different way of life from her family's, wearing the simplest of clothes and frowning on frivolities like music and dancing.

In 1800, when she was twenty, Betsy married Joseph Fry, and her own Quaker family of eleven children began to arrive. Once again children grew up to be aware of and involved in the hardships of the times because of their mother's philanthropical work inside and outside her own home. Plashet, in Essex, where the Frys lived, was like Earlham in being unusually stately for a family of Friends, but she put it to good use. As soon as they moved in she started founding schools and helping the local poor – particularly gypsies and poverty-stricken Irish immigrants. One woman who had nothing to live on was offered the loan of the family cow. 'My dear, what *will* be lent next?' her husband mildly asked as he saw the animal being led through the gate. Then came Betsy's pioneer step of starting a school for young criminals and inmates' children inside Newgate prison; and she also launched the first groups of prison visitors. As her family became old enough to go to school, she could spend more of her time on her social work. This brief outline shows how two generations of one Quaker family were almost uniquely aware of the adversity that existed in their time and of how much individuals could do to help.

Other families gave their time, money and sympathy, and taught their children to do likewise. Consciences were salved by inviting children from the workhouse or the orphanage to summer and Christmas parties. Sometimes charity had evangelistic overtones, inspiring children to wrap Biblical texts round the pennies they gave to beggars. Sometimes too the grown-ups confused children in the way they encouraged them to be charitable. At a time when the Sitwells had a shilling in pocket-money each week, they were told that they should give half of this to the poor. Osbert understood his governess 'to mean that each gesture of charity brought in a substantial and immediate return in cash from Heaven', and this impression was accidentally confirmed a few days later when his grandmother gave him a five-shilling tip. So he parted trustingly with further sixpences, and both his faith and his finances were shaken when these brought in no further celestial dividends.

During the last century a large proportion of Parliamentary seats and important public appointments went to members of the established families, and this inevitably had its effect on the children. Having a father in, say, the House of Commons or a European embassy inevitably helped to open windows on wider horizons, even if it opened them in one direction only. An overseas posting could transplant a family to India, Berlin or Canada for several years. When political colleagues came to stay, children with an interest in such things heard – and in some families took part in – stimulating conversation and discussion of state affairs. Sometimes the impact of outside events was more dramatic. One afternoon in 1872 the Wyndham children were playing, as they often did, in the gardens in front of the family's town home in Belgrave Square when they were called hurriedly back to the house. They were told the horrifying news that their uncle, Lord Mayo, who was then Viceroy of India, had been murdered by one of the convicts at a prison settlement he was visiting in the Andaman Islands. Sometimes past atrocities cast long shadows. Arthur Balfour's niece, Blanche, was devoted to him and – knowing that Lord Frederick Cavendish and Mr Burke had been assassinated there – she was tormented by anxiety when he was appointed Chief Secretary for Ireland. She tailed his two detectives, asking them endless questions, and she collected the lurid caricatures of 'Bloody Balfour' which appeared in the Irish nationalist Press. These showed him with fingers dripping with blood, and Blanche caused a flutter among her friends and their nannies when she brought them out and claimed proudly that Bloody Balfour was her uncle. But his influence went deeper than that. At Whittingehame one day she found him sorting potatoes, and her interest in politics was first aroused when he told her about the famine and poverty in Ireland. Her cousins, the Cecils, were of course interested in politics and public affairs very early. While they were still in their teens, two of the Prime Minister's older children engaged a speaker to tour the country in support of General Gordon, and they paid him out of their own money.

There are always some children who accept and take for granted what they see around them, and others who notice and question. One of the youngest and wealthiest of the questioners was Frances Maynard, known as Daisy, the future Countess of Warwick. She grew up on the three-thousand-acre Scottish estate which belonged to her stepfather, the Earl of Rosslyn, and she was very young when she began to wonder about some of the inconsistencies of the life they led. Daisy, her sister, and her five step-siblings were brought up affectionately but strictly and puritanically; in spite of the vast fortune she had been left while she was still in the nursery, she was dressed mainly in her mother's cast-off clothes and it was only on Sunday that she was allowed to take an interest in her appearance and wear her hair in curls. Even so, the day was devoted to church-going and idleness, and Daisy was quick to compare this with the hard work the coachmen and other servants had to do on the day of rest. She was disturbed at the way the congregation waited for her family to proceed first out of church, giving respectful curtseys as they went.

There were ugly things to be seen in nineteenth-century England, and these were all the more shocking for children from sheltered, luxurious homes. 'On Tuesday I saw a Tramp sitting on the side of the road, so ragged that he frightened me', wrote the future fourth Marquess of Salisbury in an early letter. The Wyndham children, on holiday at Eastbourne, also wrote about a meeting that prompted disturbing

A portrait of Frances Maynard (on her pony), the future Countess of Warwick, with her sister Blanche. It was shown at the Royal Academy in 1871. Left a vast fortune when she was still in the nursery, she was one of the few children who noticed and questioned her privileged position.

questions. They were walking to Beachy Head when they came across a little girl who was carrying a very heavy pailful of water to the cottages up there. The children stopped and asked her whether it was not dreadfully heavy. The letter does not record whether the little girl was too shy to answer, or what she said, but the question was important enough to be mentioned.

In Scotland the crofters had some very hard times, and the Balfour children saw these at close quarters. Their mother went round distributing religious tracts which she felt would be helpful, and when the American Civil War brought widespread unemployment in the cotton mills she took two girls who had lost their jobs to work in her house. Then she seems to have changed her plan of action, deciding to cut down her own staff-list and contribute the saving in wages to the Lancashire Relief Fund. This had its impact on the children, who were set to work on household jobs that now needed doing. Arthur, the future Prime Minister, cleaned the boots, the girls cooked, and the other boys did the sweeping. Some of the family properties had larger populations than the land could support, and during one journey the children were moved to a different carriage because angry tenants were expected to mob the first one.

Sometimes things looked so serious that children were moved out of the district, to another family seat. In 1831 this happened to the Granville children, though there is no record of what they thought about it. 'Did I tell you,' their mother wrote, 'that my children had been moved to Trentham owing to disturbances in Shropshire, not that it was supposed to be dangerous, but uncomfortable. They still continue, the workmen not having returned to their labour.' Marches of unemployed and hungry men alarmed the children in their big houses – sometimes stones were thrown through the large, well-polished windows. Why were the men so rough and violent, some the children asked, when Papa and Mama were always so generously giving food and clothes away? Others began to wonder why it was that they had so many homes, all so large and so beautiful, while these wild-looking people were dressed in rags, and looked so hungry and angry.

Even in quieter times the poor were always there. The first words Sir Osbert Sitwell learned were 'Rags and Bones', the cry he heard in the winter dawn from his bed in their Scarborough night-nursery. The characters he saw from the window took their places on the colourful backcloth of the elegant, spacious Sitwell scene. Osbert looked out for the rag and bone man as he did for the beggars, tramps, pedlars, organ-grinders, street singers and other 'extras' who walked across the stage. There was a negro with a limp who sold flowers, and a tramp known as Lousy Peter was teased by the boys of the town. Osbert was given a couple of pennies to throw down from the nursery window. His description of these strange misfits suggests that the children loved them for their oddity and quirkiness, that they might well have missed them if they had not been there, and that they probably lacked the empathy to project themselves inside such curious exteriors and to ask themselves whether they were perhaps deprived and unhappy in spite of their comic tricks and capers. Surprisingly enough it was the Sitwells, of all parents, who gave their children an unusually eye-opening experience: Osbert and Edith were taken on a tour of industrial works, to visit a china factory in Derby and the blazing furnaces of a steel refinery. It made a strong impression on Osbert, although he was only four at the time. His understanding of working people was mainly drawn, he always acknowledged, from the long conversations he enjoyed so much with the butler and footman in the Renishaw pantry. Like so many of the children in the big houses, during his childhood he saw the poor as 'that other nation that lived pressed into the narrow spaces between the houses of the rich'.

So the 'two nations' of the rich and the poor lived side by side in their very different ways, in accordance with an inscrutable but accepted divine plan. There are only a few records of the rich deliberately turning away from the sight of the under-privileged in their midst. Lord Melbourne used to quote to young Queen Victoria Sir Walter Scott's famous saying. 'Why do you bother the poor?' he asked, 'Leave them alone.' Some people were only too glad to take his advice. At Harrow, in the days when the Earl of Shaftesbury was there and was already dreaming his philanthropical dreams, the boys were known to be cruel and insolent to anyone they saw as socially inferior. 'The poor were never spoken of but by some contemptuous term, or looked upon as hateful boors to be fought with', one of them later remembered. But home influence was not always more gentle. Until her marriage to an earl, one baron's daughter had never been 'allowed to enter a cottage, to go where sickness and sorrow dwelt'. She had never been 'brought face to face with want or sickness'. The two nations could live next door to each other without ever looking in at each other's windows.

10

Eminent and Victorian

Not the least of the children's advantages were the brilliant people and occasions that came their way. Many parents felt that, for the girls in particular, these were a better education than regular lessons on set subjects. One of them described how she had never been taught arithmetic although her uncle was a Senior Wrangler and her aunt was a pioneer of women's education and a future Principal of Newnham College. Her mother believed, she said, in leaving her 'to pick up what I could from the great minds who surrounded my infant years'.

Often it was the quietest children who were the most deeply impressed by sparkling company and conversation. The fifth Earl of Rosebery was a solitary, rather unhappy child. 'I cannot conceal from myself that he is a terribly dull little boy. . .totally without an idea', his mother wrote in her journal when he was three. Fortunately his parents did not both feel the same way about him, as he was the favourite of his father, but he died when the boy was only four. He grew even sadder and more withdrawn, but when there were interesting visitors he came to life, sitting at table forgetful of his food, with his eyes riveted on a speaker who had caught his attention. At least he was invited to join distinguished company – unlike Osbert Sitwell who, when his mother and sixteen or so of her friends enjoyed luncheon parties together, used to be 'in attendance under the table'.

Politicians, bishops, generals, writers and royals were among those who went to stay in the great houses and made their mark on the children of their hosts. At Hatfield, the Duke of Wellington, Disraeli and Gladstone were among many outstanding visitors the children met; in this century Lord David Cecil saw Edward VII and Queen Alexandra, Lords Curzon and Kitchener, and Sir Winston Churchill when they were guests of his parents there. At Belvoir the children were brought down when someone specially interesting – Cecil Rhodes, for instance, or Lord Salisbury – was expected. John Russell, who was born in 1842, four years after his father John Russell became Prime Minister for the first time, was invited when he was twelve to go to the Palace to play with the Prince of Wales and Prince Alfred, and while he was with them he met the Queen. It was probably a trial visit, but it seems that both generations approved of him as four more invitations came along. He must have had to accept these whether he wanted to or not. The diary he kept from the age of eleven has a deadpan entry for another meeting which must have come to him because of his father. 'A boy, called prince of Condé, came to play with me', it records unenthusiastically.

Churchill and his brother Jack also met famous people through their parents. Their mother enjoyed inviting eminent politicians to the house, and Lord Rosebery, Arthur Balfour and Herbert Asquith were three future Prime Ministers whose discussions on the events of the day Churchill remembered. On one occasion Lord Randolph brought a celebrity to visit Jack at Harrow. Jack had asked his father to come and see him there, and he was not satisfied when his father sent him a pound note instead. He would much rather his father had come, he said. When at last he did come he brought General Lord Roberts with him, and they were all three given dinner by the headmaster. That was better than a pound note but what Jack, like Winston, really wanted was the chance of some intimate contact with his father. Neither of them ever got that, although Winston did get a treat in 1887, when he was twelve. He had begged to be allowed home from his prep school to take part in the Queen's Jubilee and to meet a famous friend of his uncle's, Buffalo Bill, who was coming to London with his circus. Both his requests were granted and his mother also took him on the royal yacht, where he met the Prince of Wales and the future King George V.

Two visitors who were invited more for the children than the grown-ups, though both enjoyed their company, were Edward Lear and Lewis Carroll. They were curiously alike. Both were brilliantly imaginative humorists who produced outstandingly successful books; both did these as a sideline, a recreation from their other serious career; both were unmarried and sexually unfulfilled, with complex, idiosyncratic natures which it seems they themselves did not altogether understand; both were given a special place in the affections and home of a noble family, and both had an essentially English genius – it is impossible to imagine them flowering on any other soil. Though Lear was born in 1812 and Carroll twenty years later, they flourished at roughly the same time and knew many of the same people, though it seems, surprisingly, that they never met.

Lear's introduction to the family at Knowsley came after Lord Stanley, the Earl of Derby's heir, had seen him sketching the parrots at the London Zoo, and in 1832 he invited him to draw the animals in his private menagerie. At first Lear was treated as one of the upper servants and had his meals with them; but soon it was noticed that the children kept going to the steward's room to enjoy the ridiculous rhymes and crazy drawings with which Lear delighted them. After that Lord Derby invited him to join the family and their guests – sometimes there were as many as a hundred of them – at meals and on other occasions. It was a privilege that had its drawbacks, Lear found. 'The uniform apathetic tone assumed by lofty society irks me *dreadfully*,' he wrote in a letter to a friend, adding that there was 'nothing I long for half so much as to giggle heartily and to hop on one leg down the great gallery – but I dare not.' The next best thing was to nip up to the nurseries and the far from apathetic or lofty tone of the children, who always had a warm welcome for him. They soon discovered that Lear was the undisputed *maestro* of the recently invented limerick, and in 1846 he published his *Book of Nonsense*, which consisted mainly of rhymes written by 'Derry down Derry' to amuse the grandchildren, nephews and nieces of the thirteenth Earl. It was to his great-grandchildren, grand-nephews and grand-nieces that it was dedicated, and fifteen years later an enlarged edition appeared in Lear's name.

The long gallery at Hatfield would also have been a good place to hop down. But though Lewis Carroll played the part of admired and affectionate court jester there, as Lear did at Knowsley, there is no record of his ever having felt any urge to hop. His part in the family life of the Cecils will be told later. At other houses, too, men of letters came to stay, met the children of the family and were judged by them. Not always favourably. At Hagley in 1841 Matthew Arnold was a guest of the Lytteltons and was condemned by their daughter Lucy – not for any shortcomings in his conversation but because, finding himself without a hassock in church, he did not put up with the discomfort of kneeling without one. 'Rather horrid for a strong man' was Lucy's verdict in her diary. The literary lions of the day seem to have found girls specially hard to please. The Earl of Stanhope's daughter Wilhelmina met Wordsworth when she was a young girl, and was not much impressed by him. And the Earl of Minto's young daughter Frances saw Scott when he visited her parents; but it was the day her nurse, whom she loved, had left, and she was weeping so bitterly that she 'didn't give much attention to Scott'. When Kate Stanley was taken to see Carlyle he did nothing but abuse everyone and everything, and she too was not charmed.

Augustus Hare was more on the children's wave-length. At Osterley he gathered them all round him and told them a long story, suggesting – a little immodestly, perhaps? – that the sight of them all round him as they listened might have recalled the *Decameron*. Presumably the subjects of his stories were somewhat different from Boccaccio's? He was good at suiting these to his audience, and delighted Lord Halifax's children with a blood-curdling tale about a vampire. Hare was the first author the Sitwells met, and they were suitably impressed by the awe that was created at a Renishaw tea-party when he was introduced as 'Mr Augustus Hare, the writer'. This experience was followed soon afterwards by their first meeting with a painter, when Sargent was engaged to paint a group-portrait of the family. It involved quite an upheaval as Sargent would work only in his own London studio, so the whole family migrated to the capital, taking with them furniture, a large tapestry, an earlier family portrait, pieces of sculpture, the toys the children were to play with, and their dog, so that these could all be painted. Osbert was seven and was fascinated by watching the painter at work; but Sacheverell was only two, and so of course was fidgety and restless during the endless sittings – every other day for five or six weeks. Sargent managed to hold his attention for a time by comic whistling and by endlessly repeating a limerick; but in the end even this failed, and a dummy with the same clothes and fair curls was brought along to stand in for him while he was set free.

Of all the eminent visitors to the great houses, no one had more fun with the children than the Duke of Wellington. In Brussels a few days before the Battle of Waterloo he managed to throw off the cares of a Commander-in-Chief and was seen 'sprawling on his back or on all-fours playing with the Duke of Richmond's children'. He was especially close to the wives and children of the second Marquess of Salisbury. They met at Hatfield, in London and at Walmer, where the first Lady Salisbury took the children to stay, sometimes on their own and sometimes with the Duke at Walmer Castle. He was godfather to Lord Salisbury's two oldest sons, and their mother described their excitement at the prospect of shaking hands with the Duke on one visit with their nurses and tutors to Walmer. Two years later, in 1835, their mother took the children to see him in London, where he showed them some of his treasures. He would have liked to go with them one evening, he said, to see 'King Arthur' and to share their delight in it, but something must have prevented this. The Cecil girls were often seen walking with the Duke, arm-in-arm or hand-in-hand, in his garden or on the Hatfield terrace. In April 1838 Lady Salisbury took three of the children to stay with him at Stratfield Saye, and a few days later there were five more children there – three Cecil cousins and two Grosvenors. The Duke was happy and so were the children. 'The rush of delight they make when the Duke enters the room and the way in which they surround his chair is quite *touchant*', wrote Lady Salisbury. They were never too many for him. In 1839, not long before she died, he wrote to Lady Salisbury urging her to visit him and to 'bring your daughters and Bobby and Eustace with you, or as many of them as you please'.

Seven years after his wife's death Lord Salisbury married again. His second wife was also an old friend of the Duke, and once again he saw a lot of her and her children, was godfather to them all, and each of them – including their daughter, Mary Arthur – was given his name. The second Lady Salisbury had met the Duke at her father's house in 1835, and had gone with him on a triumphal visit to Cambridge. Fifteen years later he wrote to her, reminding her of that day. There are plenty of descriptions of Wellington romping boisterously with young friends; this one shows him equally happy to share a formal occasion with a child who was then eleven. 'I perfectly recollect', he wrote, 'your standing on my knee in the open carriage and your delight with the cheers of the mob and the horses of the yeomanry galloping about the carriage, and your being particularly entertained at my being under the necessity of losing my hold of you in order to twist up my hand and salute those who were cheering.'

One daughter of a great family attracted the attention of the Prime Minister of the day, and eventually of the Queen and one of her sons, mainly because of her huge fortune. She was Daisy Maynard, the future socialist Countess of Warwick. When she was thirteen, with the promise of an annual income of over £30,000 a year, her stepfather was given office in Disraeli's government and his appointment brought many leading politicians of the day to their house. A few years later she and her sister were invited with their parents to stay at the palace of Holyroodhouse, where they joined in splendid processions through the streets of Edinburgh. The size of Daisy's fortune suggested to Disraeli, and Disraeli suggested to the Queen, that her son, Prince Leopold, might find in this charming girl a very desirable match. The Queen saw nothing against the idea and so in order to get to know young Miss Maynard and form an opinion of her, Disraeli asked her mother's and her stepfather's permission to spend an evening alone in her company.

The occasion was diplomatically stage-managed. Disraeli took the fifteen-year-old Daisy to her first play – to see Henry Irving and Ellen Terry in Shakespeare. They must have been a conspicuously incongruous couple as they sat in their big box at the Lyceum Theatre, the young girl absorbed and enchanted by the play and the acting, the old charmer watching her with his shrewd novelist's eye. Daisy described herself at that time as 'a well-tubbed, tall girl, in white muslin and blue sash, scarcely conscious of the dark, smiling face of my distinguished companion, whose pearls of wit fell for once on unheeding ears'. She evidently passed muster. Before she had officially 'come out' and so was still technically 'in the schoolroom', Lord and Lady Rosslyn received a royal command to bring her to dinner and to stay overnight at Windsor. This time it was the Queen, not the Prime Minister, who vetted Daisy and once again she came through with flying colours. But in fact the match never came to anything as the Prince's affections were engaged elsewhere, and it was eventually to be his brother the Prince of Wales to whom Daisy became attached, though not as his wife.

Contact with the royal family in a less serious context came the way of many children of the great families. All their lives they remembered the splendid occasions when royal visitors had come to their homes. In 1832 little Princess Victoria came with her mother the Duchess of Kent and her governess the formidable Baroness Lehzen to stay with the Grosvenors at Eaton Hall. After the formal reception and the speechifying the Princess must have been happy to walk around the splendid gardens with the eldest girl, who was about her age, and her younger sister. There was a colourful archery meeting and a dinner for two hundred and sixty, and then at the Princess's request the children came in and she gave them each a little present. The Grosvenor family remained on intimate terms with the Duchess and the Princess. When the King was ill and soon to die, the three eldest girls drove to St James's Palace every day with their mother to read the doctors' bulletin, and when Victoria became Queen the close link remained. They all went to Stafford House (now Lancaster House) when the Queen first went to

A children's dance at Buckingham Palace in 1859. 'All the juvenile nobility' were invited to the royal parties.

the House of Lords, to watch the procession from the garden alongside the Mall.

During the 1850s the Queen and the Prince Consort spent two nights at Stoneleigh Abbey, Lord Leigh's splendid home in Warwickshire. Big though it was, on that occasion it was so full that the younger children had to be put up elsewhere for those nights. The two eldest were squeezed into the maids' bedrooms and joined in the festivities. They were charmed by the Queen but chilled by the Prince Consort, who stiffly warded them off when they wanted to come near while the Queen planted a tree to commemorate her visit. The tree was not the only memento of the great occasion. Afterwards the children were proud to show their friends the royal lavatory which had been specially installed in a cupboard in the Queen's dressing-room.

At Fermoy in Ireland, further off the beaten track, a royal visit was correspondingly more awe-inspiring to young onlookers. When the Duke of Connaught went to Bowen's Court the children were told to wait outside till everyone was seated at the dinner-table. Then they walked in, sedately and silently in single file, as if they were coming to a church service. There they sat, in a solemn row on the horse-hair sofa, with their eyes glued to the royal shoulders. It was not a particularly genial meeting. The Duke eventually asked them their names, shook hands with each in turn, and the audience was at an end.

There were plenty of children's parties at St James's Palace. In 1828 Viscount Belgrave took his daughter Eleanor, who was eight, to one given by George IV. It was described as 'the King's ball to all the juvenile nobility. All the magnificent new suite of rooms at St James's was opened and the immense proportions of the rooms contributed to make the little pygmy gnats look more diminutive.' At twelve the younger children left – poor Eleanor had already been sent home at ten – and their places were then taken by 'young Oxonians and Cantabs... with the Misses in their teens'. The King seemed to enjoy it as much as anyone. The following year Eleanor's sister was old enough to go too, and in 1832 their seven-year-old brother went with them. When the Queen and her family were living at Buckingham Palace the children's balls were of course given there, and not at St James's.

Sometimes royal invitations were on a more personal, private footing. When Princess Victoria was in her early teens the Duchess of Kent liked her to have suitably *wohlgeboren* playmates to keep her company from time to time. In 1831 Lady Dover described the splendours and miseries

110

of one such occasion. 'We went by appointment to the Duchess of Kent yesterday with the children,' she wrote. 'It is always a nervous business. Bossy [her son] behaved very well; the little girls began by being shy, but ended by being in the most romping spirits. It is so difficult to repress them because the Princess is in such a state of enchantment when they grow rather boisterous.'

The children often had front-row views of royal processions and other state occasions. A good way, perhaps, to recapture the sound and colour of these is to follow one eminent family at the time of the Queen's Coronation celebrations in 1838. Before the great day Countess Grosvenor went 'with the coach full of children' to see the crowds, the scaffolding and the preparations at Westminster. They were told that orders had been given that no one was to be admitted, but they were more in the habit of giving than obeying orders so they 'reasoned with the Police and fetched a Herald and were at last admitted and saw it all'. The oldest boy, Hugh, Viscount Belgrave, came from his prep school to be page to his grandfather Lord Westminster and they all went to hear the Band of the Blues play at Knightsbridge Barracks, though it was so crowded that they could hardly get in. On Coronation Day, June 28, the two eldest girls went off at five in the morning with 'Peers' tickets'. Their parents, with their third daughter and Hugh in his elegant page's dress, went at half-past eight in the family coach, which followed Lord and Lady Westminster's chariot to the Abbey. They were there by ten, saw everything beautifully and arrived home at seven. But all was not yet over. That evening they took the children to see the illuminations and the fireworks and they 'came home at one in the morning all enchanted'. The next day the older children with Hugh and their parents walked about the streets and saw the Great Fair from the balcony of a house overlooking the park. There were bands playing, and long lines of tents dotted the park all the way from the Serpentine to Grosvenor Gate.

The Grosvenor children and parents must have felt very much at the heart of the great occasion – because of their links with the new Queen, and because they had been on the spot, some of them actually taking part. But there was another reason which must have made the family feel that they were almost hosts to this most royal of festivities. Or were they so used to this that they did not consciously notice that almost everything was taking place on the Grosvenor Estate, in places bearing the various family names? Their main London home, of course, was old Grosvenor House, in Park Lane, and there were other family bases in Grosvenor Square and Grosvenor Street. Both were only a few minutes' trot from Belgrave Square and Belgrave Gardens, and from Eaton Square and Wilton Place. The family had the rare distinction of bearing the name of the great church which was at the heart of the whole ceremony, to which all the horses and carriages, the guardsmen and police, the men and women of London were heading. For the scene of this Coronation, like that of others for centuries past was – of course – Westminster Abbey.

11

Sex and Sensibility

Sex must have been as important to the children and adults of that world as it always has been, but it is a difficult subject to research because many of them found it impossible to mention in conversation, let alone in writing. So it raises questions which can probably never now be answered. Memoirs, biographies and letters touch on some of them, but many of the most important are buried in old taboos, and so resist excavation and analysis. How, for instance, did nurses and parents react when a child masturbated? Often with a sharp slap or with threats of intimate surgery or future insanity – who can say with what after-effects? Gladstone's guilt about it haunted him all his life and seems to have led to his awkward addiction to the company of prostitutes; he made great efforts to avoid passing his obsession on to his children, deliberately giving them the affection, interest and freedom that he at their age had so disastrously missed. Children's nurses, of course, were usually uneducated and unmarried, trained only in the ideas of the older colleagues they had worked with at the start of their career. When another baby was expected, when puberty was due, when older brothers and sisters were about to marry, did they discuss with the children's mother what they should say? In many homes there was a dense smokescreen of silence about such delicate subjects.

Even about childbirth. Without warning, mothers disappeared into their bedrooms and were followed by medical men in dark suits, and by maids with cans of hot water, piles of linen and mysteriously covered trays. Children were told to keep quiet and not to ask questions about all the unusual to-ings and fro-ings. At last the suspense gave way to a crescendo of achievement and they would be told – sometimes actually shown – that a new baby had arrived. Often they were astounded, unable to believe that such a miracle had taken place and that their elders had evidently known all along what was going to happen. Why had they been told nothing about when, why, or how something so important to them would happen?

When such a conspiracy of silence shrouded the comparatively straightforward occasions of sex and childbirth, how much more impenetrable it must have been when complications such as incest, sadism and homosexuality reared their embarrassing heads? Byron and his family provide a good starting-point for an exploration into nineteenth-century attitudes and ideas about these and similar questions. His mother-in-law described what children were told in her young days, before the century began. It was the fashion then, she remembered, to tell children 'that Infants were found in *Parsley Beds*'. A few reconnaissance trips to the vegetable garden, backed up by some thought and observation, must surely have raised grave doubts not only about the whole mystery of procreation but also about the general trustworthiness of nurses and parents. The little girl who was told about parsley beds sounds too worldly-wise to have fallen for such an unlikely tale. She was in the habit of blackmailing a maid who was unkind to her by threatening to tell how she allowed the footman who was her lover to visit her in the nursery when she thought her charge was safely asleep.

Byron had no inhibitions about describing his own sexual precocity. 'My passions were developed very early – so early that few would believe me, if I were to state the period,' he wrote. His close friend John Cam Hobhouse told how at a very early age Byron was sitting on the lap of a pretty woman when all of a sudden he impulsively threw his arms round her neck. More unusual was his experience with the nurse who used to get into bed with him when he was about nine, playing amorously with him when her usual bedfellows failed her. The animosity between Byron and his mother seems to have prevented him telling her about this, but he did complain to the family solicitor and was consequently sent away to boarding-school. From the age of eight onwards he had a succession of childish though fervent love-affairs, mostly with pretty cousins. The first of these was a little girl called Mary Duff. In his twenties he wrote in his journal about the feeling he had had for her. 'How very odd that I should have been so utterly, devotedly fond of that girl, at an age when I could neither feel passion, nor know the meaning of the word.' Some years later the news that she had married 'nearly threw me into convulsions'. When Byron was twelve, Margaret Parker and her dark eyes prompted his 'first dash into poetry', and her death soon afterwards inspired his first published poem, 'On the Death of a Young Lady, Cousin to the Author, and very dear to him'. Though Margaret had not been his only or even his first love, and though it is an unripe little poem, it is sincere and tender:

> Yet is remembrance of those virtues dear,
> Yet fresh the memory of that beauteous face;
> Still they call forth my warm affection's tear,
> Still in my heart retain their wonted place.

But complications were on the way. When Byron was fifteen his mother let Newstead Abbey, the family seat which was now his, and the new tenant, Lord Grey de Ruthyn, was very friendly to Byron, offered him his own rooms in the house, and then cancelled out his kindnesses by making homosexual advances to him. Once again he did not manage to talk openly to his mother about this, although he wrote of it to his half-sister Augusta. They began corresponding very affectionately at about this time, having been kept apart during their childhood because their respective relations did not get on well together. They both felt estranged from those who were nearest to them and so felt all the more warmly for each other. The various question-marks about their possibly incestuous relationship date from after their childhood years, and so do not belong here.

But these suggestions did, years afterwards, touch Medora, the youngest of Augusta's seven children. Caroline Lamb went so far as to tell Byron's wife that Medora was his child; but Caroline Lamb was famous for her fanciful lies, and fortunately Medora was strikingly like Augusta's husband, Colonel Leigh. Her older sister Georgiana married in 1826, when Medora was eleven, and three years later Georgiana and her husband Henry took Medora with them when they went away to the country for Georgiana's confinement. There the plot began to thicken. Georgiana kept sending her sister to her husband's bedroom late at night when no one else was about, and took every opportunity of throwing them together. So inevitably Medora, still only fifteen, became pregnant by Henry, and the trio went abroad together so that she could give birth discreetly to her baby, who showed a similar discretion by dying a few months later. Twice more Medora became pregnant by Henry and had further secret confinements. After this – if not before? – she was no longer a child, so her story also passes beyond the scope of these pages.

Such irregular goings-on were, of course, exceptional. Most of the children saw their schoolroom years leading inexorably – by way of one or more 'seasons' for the girls – to marriage with a partner whose family and fortune was well-matched to theirs. Nurses and governesses endorsed the accepted view. One devoted nurse told the girls that she hoped they would each marry a duke – 'but he must have a loving heart'. The London season was a kind of Olympian marriage bureau and many customers found the service satisfactory. Bad choices were made when the girls were in too much of a hurry, when they were ignorant and unprepared for the sophisticated or the wicked world, and when the sudden *furore* of admiration turned the heads of pretty children who had come straight from their schoolrooms and governesses. In 1823 Harriet, the seventeen-year-old daughter of the Earl of Carlisle, still enjoyed playing with her dolls. But the time had come for her to put her hair up, let her skirts down, and launch herself on London. As the horses trotted off down the long drive, she looked back at the domed and pedimented façade of Vanbrugh's first great country mansion, the palace that had been her home. 'Goodbye, Castle Howard!' she called out of the carriage window. 'You will never see Harriet Howard again!' She knew what she wanted and she got it. Eight days later she was engaged, and before long she was a countess.

The story of Daisy Maynard's engagement opens another interesting window on the conventions of the time. She was sixteen and still in the schoolroom when she and her younger sister paid that splendid visit to Holyroodhouse with Lord and Lady Rosslyn. While they were there Lord Brooke, the Earl of Warwick's heir, fell in love with Daisy and told her mother and stepfather of his feelings. They made him promise to say nothing to Daisy until she was eighteen and 'came out'. He could call to see her at their London home occasionally but must give her no idea of his hopes. Lord Brooke kept his promise and in due course Daisy had a magnificent coming-out ball on her eighteenth birthday. But her poor admirer was still kept on ice: he was invited to the ball on condition that even then he did not propose to his beloved Daisy. The reason for all these careful tactics has already been described. Because Daisy's fortune was so vast, there was the chance of a royal marriage for her and so she must not be allowed to throw herself away on a mere earl's son. As soon as Prince Leopold told her he wanted to marry someone else, Lord Brooke was allowed to propose, was accepted and – they both lived fairly turbulently ever after. The whole procedure had been unusual. A few years later, when the Rosslyns' daughter Millicent was only sixteen, no objections were made to the Marquis of Stafford proposing to her and to their becoming engaged at once.

The accepted nineteenth-century belief that sparing the rod meant spoiling the child must be mentioned here. Whether their readiness to beat children for what now seem to be very slight offences comes under the heading of sex or of sensibility is a question that might be hard to answer. Today it seems that many of them had rather too much gusto for this particular discipline. At schools, of course, there were frequent beatings by both masters and boys, usually with a birch rod. Edward Stanley, who sounds from his letters an exceptionally unpleasant father, could write from his London home to his harrassed wife who was left far away in the country with children she found hard to manage: 'With regard to your male cubs, I should recommend a wholesome application of the birch.' On some occasions mothers did wield the rod. The second Lord Lytton was whipped – with nettles – by his mother for a lie he had never told. He had seen one of the urns on the terrace blown over and broken, but she insisted it was he who had done it.

Another surprising flagellant was kind Lord Melbourne, whose obsession with whipping has only lately come to light. The subject became something of a joke between him and Susan Churchill, and it seems it never damaged their affection for each other. Lord Melbourne remembered whipping Susan only once – 'for disobedience and she never disobeyed me any more'. Years after her marriage Susan mentioned it to him in a letter. She remembered, she said, 'as though it was yesterday, the *execution*, then being thrown in a corner of a large couch...You used then to leave the room and I remember your coming back and saying "Well cocky does it smart still?" at which of course I could not help laughing instead of crying.' He kept returning to the subject. When Susan was about twelve, Lord Melbourne asked her if she was ever whipped at school. No, she answered; she would not allow any such thing. Her guardian was 'shocked' to hear this but, he said, he could not take the trouble to move her to a different school where she would be 'under proper discipline'. He made a similar point in a letter to his mistress, Lady Brandon, about public criticism of a girl being given a beating. 'It is rarely that so minute and circumstantial a history of a flagellation is put on record,' he wrote in 1831, surely not without some relish. 'We live in strange times when a girl of thirteen cannot be whipped at a boarding school without its being made a subject of description in the newspapers.' There is no suggestion of guilt or reticence in his voice when he discusses such things; but ideas have changed so much that it is hard to judge or analyse the motives and feelings of over a hundred years ago.

The same is true of 'the love that dare not speak its name'. It has already been seen that Lord Berners got into trouble for wanting to change his toy horse for a doll – almost certainly because the grown-ups were at least subconsciously worried about homosexuality. Or was it no more than everyday disapproval of behaviour that did not even attempt to conform with the accepted stereotype, like Lady Hester Stanhope wearing the dress of a Muslim chieftain, or even the mildly masculine conversation and appearance of the third Marquess of Salisbury's two daughters? '*Il n'y a que des hommes dans cette famille-là*', a French diplomat said after a visit to Hatfield. Homosexuality was of course rife at boys' schools, but how was it treated when it turned up – the real thing, not just a passing adolescent phase – in the home? It seems that no one tried to check or to monitor in any way the passionate love that Violet Keppel and Vita Sackville-West had for each other. They were free to talk, kiss, declare their feelings, stay in Scotland and in Italy together, dress up, chase each other down the passages of an ancient Scottish castle, and spend the whole night together. No eyebrows were raised when Violet filled Vita's room with tuberoses, and when she was sixteen Violet evidently felt free – though why did she write in French? – to send Vita a passionate letter which Nigel Nicolson has included, in translation, in his book about his parents' marriage. It was probably the strength of their characters and their feelings, as well as the exceptional freedom – and a certain amount of grown-up indifference – in which both grew up, that made such a brave statement possible:

> I love you, Vita, because I have had to fight for you so hard. I love you because you never gave me back the ring I lent you. I love you because you will never capitulate. I love you for your fine intelligence, for your literary ambition, for your innocent flirtatiousness. And I love you because you never seem to doubt my love. I love in you what I know is also in me, that is, imagination, a gift for languages, taste, intuition, and a mass of other things. I love you, Vita, because I have seen your soul.

Vita Sackville-West at Knole. She said that when she was ten she was 'an unsociable and unnatural girl with long black hair and long black legs, and very short frocks and very dirty nails and torn clothes'.

12

To and Fro

Families spent a lot of time on the road. Many of them had more than one country house – the Cavendishes had five as well as Chatsworth and their London houses – and so were always travelling to stay in other places. The great dynasties were linked by an intricate network of intermarriages which brought uncles, aunts and cousins to stay with each other in great gatherings of the clan, and these also took place when the younger members visited their grandparents, usually in the main ancestral home. The many families with Parliamentary connections followed an annual migration-cycle, moving off to town in about February and staying on through the London season. This began in April, when fox-hunting was over for the year, and went on till Parliament adjourned in July. None of this had much to do with the children, of course, but some of them went with their parents to London while others were left in the country with nurses and governesses – sometimes with their mother too – to be conveniently out of their father's way. Edward Stanley, the disagreeable father who has been heard recommending a 'wholesome application of the birch' for his wife's 'male cubs', made no bones about his dread of having his family with him in town. 'Their increased and increasing malignity will not make the house full in London more agreeable', he wrote fondly to his wife. Perhaps his words had their desired effect, as she answered with a reassurance that she had plans to 'locate the children without your being aware they are in the house'.

Great seasonal occasions like Christmas, the New Year and grouse-shooting brought the families together and set the pattern for the whole year's comings and goings. When Lord Salisbury wrote to engage a new tutor for his sons, he explained that they spent about five months every year in town, dividing the rest between Cranborne in Dorset and Hatfield. From October to February they were based on Hatfield, where on most weekends there were parties – mainly official ones – lasting from Saturday to Monday. But there was still time for family get-togethers. Lewis Carroll found forty children and grown-ups staying in the house for a children's ball when he arrived on one New Year's Eve. After the children had grown up and grandchildren began to arrive, a separate table was laid in the dining-room for them, and it came to be known as the 'Buttons' table.

For the Sitwell children 'home' always meant Renishaw, though they enjoyed long visits to London and to their grandparents. The Earl and Countess of Londesborough, their mother's parents, entertained five or more branches of the family at a time with all their children and nurses in great splendour at Scarborough. The grandparents provided endless expeditions and delights for all ages, none more exciting than going for a drive at a spanking pace with Lord Londesborough in his buck-board, 'a dashing equipage...balanced precariously on two enormous wheels and drawn by, one would have said, a permanently bolting horse'. They drove part of the way and then, at a certain point, would find a groom waiting to take over both horse and carriage so as to meet grandfather and children when they had walked up one hill and down another.

Months each year were spent visiting the magnificent houses which belonged to hospitable relatives and friends. Augusta Byron during her childhood used to spend the season in London and then was taken on a round of visits. They made courtesy calls on the young princesses, then went to the Devonshires at Chatsworth and the Rutlands at Haddon Hall nearby before going on to Yorkshire to stay with Augusta's cousins at Castle Howard. In the 1830s the Gower family made a similar tour on their way home from Scotland, staying at inns at the few places where there were no relations in a splendid castle to welcome them. The inns where they put up have not been recorded, but their journey southward included a visit to the Tankervilles at Chillingham Castle, to the Duke of Northumberland at Alnwick Castle, to their mother's old home at Castle Howard and their own family seat at Lilleshall. At about the same time the Grosvenors went on a parallel circuit, enjoying house-parties at Knowsley, Hawarden, Tatton Park, Castle Howard, Bowood and Badminton. The Gladstones, unlike most of their relations and friends, went by public transport when in 1853 they travelled to Scotland with their six children – aged between one and thirteen – and stayed *en route* with the Duke of Argyll at Taymouth, Lord Aberdeen at Haddo and the Duke of Sutherland at Dunrobin. The children had cousins and castles waiting to welcome them everywhere.

The way the families travelled was very varied and makes colourful reading today. In 1837 Lord and Lady Salisbury set off with three children by steamer from London to Margate, going on from there to Walmer in a fly. The following year, after all the junketings following the Queen's Coronation, Lord and Lady Grosvenor with four children and two servants embarked for Invergordon in the Duke of Richmond's steamer. It was awaiting them at its London mooring and had arrived there from Scotland that same morning. They were all exhausted by the festivities, settled happily in the large cabin with its eight places and two divisions, and were delighted to go straight to bed. When the family travelled between London and their country home at Eaton, near Chester, at first the children usually went in the Grosvenor coach, which was drawn by four horses and was also used for formal occasions in town. But after more children had arrived, the younger ones with their governesses and two nurserymaids went in the coach while their parents travelled more peacefully in the open britchka, sometimes with one child with them, and with two servants in the dickey, an extra folding seat at the back.

It was quite a brave venture to travel to their grandfather's Scottish castle with a family of young children, as the Duke of Argyll's daughter and son-in-law did every Christmas in the early years of their marriage. They went by steamboat from Greenock to Lochgoilhead, where they took the mail coach; the children were stowed inside where it was dark and warm, while their mother sat on the box-seat. On one dramatic occasion there were handcuffed prisoners inside the coach with them, on their way to the Assizes at Inveraray. The last lap of the journey to the castle was in an open steam ferry across Loch Fyne, where both waves and wind could be wild.

But new ideas were on the way. In 1838 the Grosvenors had their first taste of travelling by the new-fangled railroad, setting off with their three eldest children at half-past seven in the morning from Euston Square to visit their grandfather at Eaton. It was a historic moment, but by the middle of the century everyone had become used to it. Trains then went slowly enough for the passengers to be seen from the trackside, and one October day in 1851 four of the Stanley children had the thrill of making their way to a nearby point in order to 'see the Queen pass, which supreme felicity they had, & saw a child at the window'.

By train too, as in the old coaching days, many parents found they had a more restful ride if the children and their nurses were behind a soundproof barrier, in another carriage. On arrival, the railway station

The Wyndham children in their pony-cart with their nurse and governess in 1874. Lady Leconfield, their mother, is standing behind Neddy.

On a steamer in the Highlands in 1871. Many families travelled to Scotland every year, and lochs were crossed in open steam ferries.

was sometimes still a good way from the house they were going to and special arrangements had to be made for the last lap of the journey. The Wyndhams needed a hired omnibus as well as a cart for their luggage, so a letter had to be sent ahead to the station-master to make sure these would be ready for them. The annual migration of the Balfour family from London to Whittinghame in Scotland is a good example of one of these great strategic upheavals. There were no corridor trains then, so the parents, all the children, two nurses, their mother's maid and their large collie dog crowded into a reserved third-class carriage of the Flying Scotsman at King's Cross. The journey to Berwick-on-Tweed took eight hours, with only one twenty-minute stop that gave them time to leave the train. That was at York, where they made a dash for lavatories and refreshment. The nurses had with them a 'small folding receptacle', made of rubber, for the children's use 'in case of urgent need'. The family were all patriotic Scots and on the northward journey they cheered loudly when they were half way across the Tweed, hissing disapprovingly at the same point on the way home.

At Berwick they changed into a slow train for East Linton, where they were delighted to find the Whittinghame carriages waiting for them, with old Sailor harnessed in the wagonette and a pair of horses to draw the children in the brougham. For Blanche the excitement of arriving was not over till the next morning. The first thing she always did then was to make her way from the nursery wing to pay a visit to the little old housekeeper, Mrs Anderson, known to them all as 'Fairy'. They were old friends, and Fairy used to delight Blanche by tying a bunch of grapes under the belly of the rocking-horse so that she would find it as soon as she woke up. Even after they had arrived safely at Whittinghame there were still dangers on the road. One day they were crossing a ford in the wagonette when the horses started to plunge, and one of them fell. The carriage overturned, tipping Blanche, her little brother, their aunt and the coachman into the chilly river.

Some visits were more memorable than others. In 1835 Lord de la Warr and his family stayed at Walmer for several weeks, and one morning they all went to a breakfast at Walmer Castle with the Duke of Wellington. Their daughter Mary was eleven at the time and it was an occasion she would not soon forget. The King and Queen of the Belgians, the Duchess of Kent and Princess Victoria were there as well. The Duke, as always, enjoyed talking to children. 'I spoke to the great General and Hero of Waterloo very often', Mary recorded, little knowing that before long, both before and after she became Marchioness of Salisbury, she would have many more conversations with him. More everyday occasions were the visits to the seaside, where children stayed with nurses and governesses, sometimes with their mother too, and on rare occasions even with their father. They stayed in 'lodgings' which were usually very different from the splendid homes they were used to, or else they rented houses for two or three weeks or months. These were of all sorts and sizes, usually chosen because they were right on the beach where the healthy sea air could blow straight in through the windows. Not many of the rented houses were as small and primitive as the Sussex cottage where the Duke of Rutland's family stayed, summer after summer, from the time when Lady Diana Cooper was six. It was, she says, a big change from Belvoir Castle. They bathed straight into the sea from a bathing-machine, but there was only an earth closet, and 'one old dear to do everything'.

Foreign travel came the children's way for various reasons. In 1841 the Stanleys were thinking of letting their London house and wondered where they should go. What would be best for the children? Lady Stanley, their grandmother, recommended going abroad. 'Education, society, everything' was as good there as in England, and much cheaper; and to prove her point she instanced one mother they all knew who had travelled around 'in expensive places' with nine children for under £3,000. That was a lot of money in those days and she does not mention how long it lasted the ten of them – with their retinue, of course.

Families also went abroad for the parents' or children's health or to cheer them up after an illness or death in the family. After their mother died the Gore children were all taken by their father to stay with their grandmother who had rented a villa at Cannes. After the Earl and Countess of Carlisle agreed to go their separate ways the Countess went with some of her children, when they were still quite young, to Italy and – surprisingly, considering the scale on which they lived in England – wherever she stayed she took great trouble to find cheap lodgings for them. There was no cheese-paring about Vita Sackville-West's visits to Paris, where she went every summer with her mother and grandfather to stay with Sir John Murray Scott in his two exquisite, treasure-packed homes. Sometimes English visitors repeated the pattern of their social life at home, walling themselves in behind class and nationality barriers and carefully avoiding the company of local people or anyone else who for one reason or another was to be kept at arm's length. '*Ils ne sont pas de notre monde*', they would say, and after that final verdict there would be no contact for the family with them or their children.

Several families had an exciting introduction to the splendours of Continental social life. In 1830 the Earl and Countess of Minto had an impressive family of five sons and five daughters between the ages of three and eighteen. When they were in Paris some of them went to a magnificent ball at the Palais Royal. They were one of the families who travelled partly because of their father's job; early in 1832 they went to Berlin, where he had been appointed Minister. They were abroad far less long than the three sons of Lord William Russell, the British Minister to the Court of Württemberg, who spent almost all their childhood on the Continent. For the comparatively short journeys Lord Salisbury made after he became Foreign Secretary in 1878 there was no need for his children to go with him, but his oldest son, who was still at school, did in fact go with him to the Congress of Berlin that year, and his eldest son and daughter went with him to Constantinople, visiting Paris, Berlin, Vienna and Rome on the way.

Few of the English families cut more of a dash on the Continent than the Earl and Countess of Grosvenor. In June 1835 they set off with their three eldest daughters and their son, Miss Reilly the senior governess, two maids, a manservant and a courier. They took with them a coach and a britchka and went by sea to Hamburg, where they were graciously welcomed by the King and all the royal family. Because there were plenty of good teachers for the children there they decided to spend the winter at Stuttgart, where the Württemberg royal family gave them another warm welcome and the children found good English friends in the three Russell boys. Among the occasions that both parents and children specially enjoyed were the days they spent helping to bring in the grape harvest in October, when they joined in the work and in the eating of sausages and exploding of gunpowder with which they all celebrated.

The next month the city was deep in snow. The children learned to skate and were taken to the opera, the theatre and the circus. The following February they all set off for Italy, where they stayed in Rome and Genoa, coming back by way of Paris and arriving home in Grosvenor Square in August. That was all for the time being, but four years later the parents took the four eldest girls – not their son, who was then at Eton – for a twelve-month Mediterranean cruise in a 200-ton yacht which Lord Grosvenor chartered.

Then, as now, the Riviera attracted well-to-do travellers from England. The drawing shows children with their parents on the *Promenade des Anglais*, Nice, in 1881.

Perhaps travelling was in their blood. They were related to the Leighs, who were perhaps the most flamboyant of all the travelling families. When Chandos Leigh spent three years wandering round the Continent with his children, he took three coaches with him – one for himself and his wife, one for the schoolroom children and staff, and one for the nursery. There was a historic moment when the Grand Duke Constantine came across their cavalcade on the Riviera. He was used to impressive sights, but even he was stirred by the Leighs. '*Toute l'Angleterre est en route*', he said as he watched them go on their way.

13

Castles and Abbeys

> I remember, I remember,
> The house where I was born ...

Many people do, of course, whether the house happens to be one of a row of miners' cottages, a factory worker's tower-block flat, or a splendid ancestral home like Chatsworth or Bowood. Children accept their early surroundings and circumstances, and are slow to recognize that they are in any way exceptional. Many of the children of the great houses, however, do seem to have had a specially warm affection for their home. Sidney Herbert wrote to his mother about the beautiful house that Inigo Jones and James Wyatt built for his ancestors: 'There is not a spot about Wilton now which I do not love as if it were a person.' Vita Sackville-West said that when she was a child she never knew what it was to live in ugly rooms. Her feelings for Knole, like Sidney Herbert's, were personal and passionate; the experience of living in – and belonging to – such a poetic, historic place must have been all-important, gently and gradually moulding her to match its mood.

In 1893, when she was only eighteen months old, she was seen courageously trotting across the Green Court on her own, followed at a respectful distance by a footman. That picture suggests that a small child might well be overwhelmed by the vastness, let alone any other quality of the place. But it seems that she always found it friendly as well as wonderful. The following year there was a day when no one knew where she was: she had had the idea of finding her way back to her nursery alone, wandering across the gardens and through the endless galleries and rooms. Years later, on the night before her wedding, she wrote about her childhood and the jewel in which it had been set:

> Pictures and galleries and empty rooms,
> Small wonder that my games were played alone;
> Half of the rambling house to call my own,

129

And wooded gardens with mysterious glooms . . .
This I remember, and the carven oak,
The long and polished floors, the many stairs,
Th'heraldic windows, and the velvet chairs,
And portraits that I knew so well, they almost spoke.

George Wyndham, who was born in 1863, felt as warm an affection for Cockermouth Castle, one of his family homes. It managed to be splendid and intimate at the same time, as it was a smallish Georgian house built inside the ruins of the surrounding castle, which presided over the river Derwent and the town of Cockermouth. His childhood was spent between the castle and three other beautiful houses – at Wilbury in Wiltshire, at Belgrave Square in London, and at Petworth where they stayed until the death of old Lord Leconfield in 1869. On their Petworth visits, in spite of the number and size of the rooms in the house, the three children, their nanny – who had the resounding surname of Horsnaill – and a nurserymaid were allowed only two small rooms, where they had to spend all their nights and days.

A great house and the all-important fact of belonging to it as it belonged to them gave children an early sense of their history and dignity. Even at the tender age of four years old. There was a remarkable occasion at Chatsworth just before the century began, when the Duke of Devonshire was ill, and unable to review the Derbyshire Militia as he had hoped. What was to be done? His four-year-old son, little Hartington, stepped into the breach and took his father's place at this formidable ceremony. With pardonable pride his mother described the scene in a letter to the child's grandmother.

> You cannot think how pretty it was to see his little figure in the regimentals standing in the middle of the field and taking off his hat as they saluted him, his little fair locks blowing about by the wind. Of his own accord he desired to give the soldiers bread and cheese and ale. They were delighted with him, and the officers gave us a very pretty breakfast.

Lord David Cecil had a similar triumph when he was six. Early in the present century, he stood in for his father, the Marquess of Salisbury, at the Hatfield Tenants' Dinner. All around him in the splendid Marble Hall sat the Hatfield tenants. They had raised their glasses to drink his mother's health, and he stood on the High Table, dressed in a blue satin

Stately homes sometimes called for stately clothes. These three glum little girls, booted and muffed on the front steps of Longleat in 1871, are the daughters of the fourth Marquess of Bath.

tunic with a lace collar and a long fringed sash, to thank them on her behalf.

Osbert Sitwell did find Renishaw frightening, with its great candle-lit rooms, shadowy corners and ghosts. There were also ghosts at Newstead Abbey, which Byron inherited when he was ten. Fortunately he was delighted with its great rooms, its quiet cloisters, and with the ghosts – an ancestor in the library, and a headless monk. Another child who had already lived in several other houses before coming to the Abbey that was to be her home was the future Lady Ottoline Morrell. Her father was a distant cousin of the Duke of Portland, and it was only through what her biographer calls 'a series of dynastic mishaps' that he became heir. But he died before the Duke did, and things looked bleak for Ottoline, her mother and her brothers. They moved into a more modest house, cut down their staff, and for a time the children had fewer toys. In due course the dukedom, with Welbeck Abbey and the other estates, was inherited by the old Duke's half-brother and it was only on his death that the family came into their fortune and moved to Welbeck. Ottoline was six, and she and her eleven-year-old brother were taken to Cremer's toyshop in Regent Street and told they could choose whatever they liked. Two weeks later they made their way to the vast Abbey.

It was an extraordinary experience for them all. The fifth Duke had been a capricious eccentric who had indulged his taste for crazy large-scale building schemes. He had built a roller-skating rink for his servants, and huge underground rooms and tunnels – one was a mile and a half long, and wide enough for two carriages to drive side by side in it all the way to Worksop station. It was a strange inheritance for young children. Did it perhaps help to make Ottoline the flamboyant, self-dramatizing person she eventually became? Her mother told her the family history as she showed her portraits of her ancestors and their possessions. These included Henry VIII's dagger, the pearl ear-ring that Charles I wore at his execution, and a casket once used by William of Orange – in which Ottoline in her schoolroom days kept her letters.

Ambitious alterations and 'improvements' did not always make the houses comfortable to live in. Eaton Hall, the Grosvenors' seventeenth-century home, was not large or imposing enough for the second Earl, so when he succeeded in 1802 he set to work to rebuild it in the Gothic style. But it was still icy in winter. The Earl also changed his main London base from Millbank to Mayfair, where he moved in to Gloucester House, renaming it Grosvenor House. His son, Lord

Arthur, known as Douro, and Charles, the Duke of Wellington's sons, with their cousin at Stratfield Saye not long after the Battle of Waterloo. One of the earliest paintings to show boys wearing Eton suits.

Belgrave, and his family lived nearby at 13 Grosvenor Square until – as their numbers quickly grew – they moved into a double-sized house at No. 15. So the whole family were living on the Grosvenor estate, and that part of Mayfair seemed almost their private village. When Lord Grosvenor died in 1845 it was a relatively simple move for the family to migrate to Grosvenor House while the dowager Lady Grosvenor settled in the home they had left.

A house is a symbol of shelter and security, and the sight of a beautiful old place being pulled down is as dismaying as that of a fine old tree being felled. Edward Lytton visited Knebworth, his family's sixteenth-century home, when he was eight, soon after his grandfather's death in 1811. The next time he saw it, workmen had started to pull it down. His mother had inherited the vast building and had decided to demolish three of its four wings. The sale of a family home is almost equally unsettling for the children who have lived in it. When Lady Diana Cooper was six, the Bedfordshire house where the family had lived was sold at about the same time as their London house in Bruton Street. The two moves started up a train of fears in her. Was her father going bankrupt? Were her parents going to get divorced? The firm foundations of life were shaken, though she might perhaps have been reassured by the fact that a fine new house was being bought for them in Arlington Street.

Changes were more often up the scale than down it. But moves even to grander homes called for adaptability. In the 1870s Middleton Park in Oxfordshire was the home of the seventh Earl and Countess of Jersey and their children; their favourite house, at Osterley Park, exquisitely decorated and furnished by Robert Adam, was occupied by the Duchess of Cleveland. When she died, they decided to move in. It was courageous though perhaps not altogether wise to let a family of rumbustious young children romp around those elegant rooms. They did their lessons in the Etruscan Room, and in moments of boredom amused themselves by peeling the delicate paint off the chairs which Adam had so carefully matched with the colours of the walls and ceilings. At least their vandalism was done on the quiet, unlike the rowdy games of indoor cricket which, it will soon be seen, the Lyttelton children played in the historic gallery at Hagley. At Hatfield, too, the young Cecils played boisterous games of billiard fives in a room which glowed with seventeenth-century panelling, used the cradle in which the infant Charles I had slept as a stage property for their charades, and rode up and down the marble floor of the Armoury – which is the main entrance to the house – on tricycles with iron wheels.

Imaginative children can transform even the stateliest houses into challenging adventure-playgrounds. The future Duchess of West-minster spent her childhood in a 'grace and favour' home in the Saxon Tower at Windsor Castle, and after that they moved to another inside St James's Palace. The royal family and the Court were all around them, but the children took all such things in their stride. Loelia and her brother used to enjoy climbing through the narrow skylight window of their attic and scrambling all over the roofs of the palace. A favourite game from that height was to squeeze water from a dripping sponge on to the sentries below them, to make them think it had started to rain. But that trick was their undoing. A complaint was made and the attic was put out of bounds.

Nurseries and schoolrooms were usually tucked away, tactfully and thankfully, at the top of the houses, where they sometimes shared a floor with servants' bedrooms. Often there was a door which acted as a useful sound-deadener at the foot of the stairs which led to the children's quarters. The shortest legs should have the most stairs to climb, it was generally agreed. At Hardwick there were ninety-seven steps, counted by the children as they scampered and puffed their way up them from the ground floor to their part of the house. Early in this century the young Cavendishes ran up and down them several times a day. Every time they needed a change of shoes, or a pair of gloves for their afternoon walk, up they had to go. The lift was for grown-ups only. Hardwick was near to Chatsworth and the boys rode there on their ponies while the rest of the family drove over there in a covered wagon – horse-drawn, of course – sitting back-to-back in it.

Of all the splendid Continental houses the children visited on their journeys abroad, few could compare with the two Paris homes which Vita Sackville-West visited every summer. They belonged to the bountiful and fabulously rich Sir John Murray Scott, and were full of the exquisite French furniture and tapestries which had belonged to Sir Richard Wallace, whose magnificent treasures can now be seen in the Wallace Collection in London. Sir John had a huge flat in central Paris, on the corner of the Boulevard des Italiens and the rue Laffitte, and for a sensitive, appreciative child just to stay there must have been an education in French *douceur de vivre*. From the fruit to the chandeliers, everything was exquisite and was cared for as it deserved to be by a full

135

complement of skilled and devoted staff. They even included a full-time *lingère*, whose time and expertise were well directed, for Vita noticed that every sheet in the flat was like the finest cambric pocket handkerchief. Sir John had a second, equally delightful Paris home, La Bagatelle, in the Bois de Boulogne. On sunny afternoons he used to drive them there, and Vita found delicious little lakes, with bridges, diminutive islands and cool caves where she played.

What better compost could there have been in which to plant a vigorous literary talent? Ever since she was twelve, Vita wrote and wrote for hours on end, and she actually finished eight full-length novels (one of which was in French) and five plays. She was at home in England, Scotland and France, yet almost all her early writings were inspired, not by the glamour of Parisian life or London society, nor by the wild moors and glens of Scotland that she enjoyed so much, but by Knole and the history of the Sackvilles.

Nurseries and schoolrooms were usually at the top of the house behind a soundproof door.
This one was at Minley Manor, Hampshire (1899).

14

Rebels and Conformists

After looking at so many aspects of the lives of the children of the great country houses, the most important of all still has to be tackled. What did they and their parents actually think? About their own lives, about the children, about the world they lived in? How open-minded were they? Which of them let their children make up their own minds about important matters? Which of them tried – all too often successfully – to force sons and daughters to swallow their parents' ideas? How did the children arrive at the ideas which were to inspire and direct their later lives?

Sometimes there is no clue to follow. While he was still at school Byron had great aspirations and a strong sense of his own destiny. Did these come from his genetic code, from his need to assert his own individuality in opposition to his mother's? Or perhaps partly from the distress he felt at his lameness? At all events, it was during the time he described in one poem as his 'hot youth' and in another as his 'repugnant youth' that he wrote to his mother about his dreams. 'I can, I will cut myself a path through the world or perish in the attempt ...I will carve myself the passage to Grandeur, but never with Dishonour.'

It seems that writers often have early ambitions. The first Lord Lytton said that he could not remember a time when he did not have 'a calm and intimate persuasion that, one day or other, I was to be somebody, or do something'. His certainty was confirmed by a strange incident. Once when he was very young he was out with his nurse when they were stopped by a madman. He lifted the little boy in his arms, prophesied that he would be greater than his father and then – went off and drowned himself. His dramatic words and action gave Lytton 'the impulse to be ambitious'.

A future career – though not the one he finally settled on – was suggested to Churchill far more casually. On one of the rare occasions when their father spared time to talk to them, he found his two sons playing with their toy soldiers. That gave him an idea. Would Churchill like to go into the Army, he asked? Yes, Winston answered at once, and his father took him at his word, young though he was. Lord Randolph was not usually quick at falling in with his sons' wishes, and Churchill was told later that he agreed so promptly on this occasion because he had decided that Winston was not clever enough for the Bar. He was also not often careful about sparing their feelings and he might well have told him to his face what a poor opinion he had of him. There was not much communication between them. At the time of Lord Randolph's own political failure, he and his wife were careful not to mention it in front of the boys or the servants. But it seems that the boys sensed it.

One child whose interests and ambitions were roused by personal affection and admiration is the present Earl of Longford. His hero was an uncle, who handed on to him his own enthusiasm for sport and his interest in under-privileged people, introducing him to an East End boys' club which at once appealed to him. Even in the nursery he was fascinated by politics and newspaper reports of them. He used to question grown-ups about the statesmen of the day. Was Lloyd George a good man? How about Asquith? And Carson? History does not record what answers he received, but the Pakenhams were among the comparatively rare families which were capable of throwing up an occasional non-conformist – surely a healthy sign of vigour and toler-ance. The children were brought up partly in Ireland and partly in England as Protestants and Conservatives, and yet while he was still a young man Lord Longford changed his faith and his ideas, becoming what he has remained ever since, a Roman Catholic and a Socialist. It has been suggested that the necessary flexibility was encouraged by the family's somewhat ambivalent position when the children were in the nursery and the schoolroom. Wherever they were they might seem – and perhaps feel – outsiders: English in Ireland, and Irish in England; rich to the poor, and poor to the rich; rustic in London, and sophisticated in the country; known to be well-born, and yet clearly nothing to do with the smart set. At all events it was an unusually stimulating and productive nursery.

Children who had an active politician in the family, whether or not he was eminent, naturally had a specially early introduction to public life. Not many six-year-olds have a telegram addressed personally to them to announce an election result. This happened to Blanche Balfour in 1886, when her mother had been canvassing for A. J. Balfour, Blanche's uncle, and knew how interested she would be to hear that he had been returned – though by only a narrow squeak, with a majority of thirteen votes. The trouble about growing up in a political family was that all too often the children were shown the world from only one point of view. The first Earl of Leicester's grandfather took him on his knee when he was very young and said to him, 'Now remember, Tom, as long as you live, never trust a Tory.' And it seems he never did. In another cocksure Whig family a young daughter had drawn her own conclusions from the grown-up conversations she had heard. 'Mamma,' she asked, 'are Tories born wicked, or do they grow wicked afterwards?' Her mother's answer was as prompt as it was positive. 'They are born wicked', she said. 'And they grow worse.' The Cecils were more subtle. Lord Salisbury told his children that they must make up their own minds about things. He always showed them the opposite point of view, though not perhaps without giving them a gentle prod in what, to him, was the right direction. He gave them an anti-Christian article to read. 'Read what rubbish these people write!' he said as he handed it to them.

Many parents were careful to keep their children out of range of what they considered to be undesirable company or subversive ideas. Old Lady Stanley strongly disapproved of granddaughters who were 'so near grown-up' – they were all in their teens – being present at their mother's dinner-table when a divorcee was among the guests. The Rosslyns were equally careful when they went to London for the season. The children were given their meals at a table on their own, where the talk of the town could not reach them. In the country, too, they were not encouraged to meet or talk with the men and women of the world, the scholars, wits and racing men who often came to stay.

Many years were to pass before sexual *mores* loosened up again and came nearer to the freer, more relaxed mood of the eighteenth century. When Vita Sackville-West was thirteen she was quite at home in the ways of fashionable Edwardian society. When she went to play with her friend Violet Keppel, whose mother was the King's mistress, there was sometimes an anonymous little one-horse brougham outside in the street, and the butler would ask her to wait below for a moment. 'One minute, miss,' he would say, without mentioning any name. 'A gentleman is coming downstairs.' The new century and the new monarch had brought with them new ideas, and slowly but surely these rubbed off on the children.

It was not only the contamination of unconventional sexual behaviour that parents tried to spare them. For some time the Gladstone family were not allowed to meet their father's sister, because she was an opium addict and – even worse, perhaps, in their eyes? – finally decided to be received into the Roman Catholic church. The Countess of Carlisle went so far as to forbid one of her younger children to meet an elder brother who had got into debt. Yet she herself had grown up in the Stanley family, which was known for its independence of mind and the variety of its religious beliefs. One of her brothers was a declared agnostic; a sister was 'Broad Church'; another brother began as a High Church clergyman, was then received into the Roman Catholic church, and eventually became a bishop and domestic chaplain to the Pope; and to cap it all, her eldest brother was a Muslim. But not even that ecumenical family grounding taught Rosalind Howard to let her children have their own opinions.

In most families the conditioning of daughters was a non-stop, home-based process, aimed at instilling the 'right' ideas, manners and – eventually – choice of husband. This last objective was achieved mainly by narrowing the social range so that 'undesirable' suitors simply did not turn up. Occasionally someone was honest enough to look the subject squarely in the face and put flesh on accepted conventions by stating them in words, even in writing. When Mary Glynne, who later married George Lyttelton, refused Lord Gairlie's proposal, her aunt put things in a nutshell for her. 'Women are not like men,' she wrote, 'they cannot chuse, nor is it creditable or lady-like to be what is called in love; I believe that few, very few, well-regulated minds ever have been and that romantic attachment is confined to novels and novel-readers, the silly and numerous class of young persons ill-educated at home or brought up in boarding-schools.'

The great question of how children's minds should be guided led to some very varied parental thinking on the subject of boarding-school for boys. (As has been seen, there was no question of any such thing for girls at least until the end of the century.) The Russell family had strong ideas on the matter though curiously enough it was Lord William Russell, whose three sons never went near a public school, who sang such a *fortissimo* hymn of praise to them. In 1822 he wrote to his brother, the Marquess of Tavistock:

I cannot tell you how happy it has made me to hear that Russell is to go to a public school – be it Eton or Westminster or elsewhere a public school is what is necessary & is that which will add to his happiness hereafter & be a source of great satisfaction to yourself. I grant that the system of education is bad – that a boy learns little, that there are many objections to a public school – but it fits a boy to be a man – to know his fellow creatures – to love them – to be able to contend with the difficulties of life – to attach friends to him – to take a part in public affairs – to get rid of his humours & caprices & to form his temper and manners – to make himself loved and respected in the world.

But when should a boy go to school? The Duke of Bedford advised Lord William to start thinking about sending his eldest son when he was eight years old. He himself had been sent at seven, and Lord William and his brother had gone at that age. But it was too early, and nine would perhaps be better. The Duke had, he said, 'a dislike for home tutors' and felt that boys should be 'removed from home at a certain age'. Yet a few months later he was writing to Lord William's wife that 'a public school in England is one of the greatest evils I know of, but I fear . . . it is a necessary evil'. Her husband answered that in England people thought that manliness and character could not exist without school education, but for his part he thought nothing could be further from the truth. To prove his point he asked his wife to consider his own two young brothers. They had been sent to school and were well grounded in the classics, but 'in everything else they are little savages, with minds not elevated above the grooms'. Going away to school had brought them a further disadvantage: 'As for their father and mother, they scarcely know them.' A child's greatest blessing, Lord William felt sure, was to have 'an attentive mother, the greatest misfortune is to have no mother, or a negligent or foolish or vicious mother. The mother forms the child's first principles, & if they are well grounded, they never desert him thro life.' As a wife, Lady William did not altogether come up to her husband's requirements, but as a mother he felt no one could be better, and for that and other reasons he was strongly against sending their sons away to school.

Only a few public schools, of course, were considered 'suitable for noblemen's sons'. Eton headed the list, though it too came in for serious criticism. Early in the century there was a custom there for boys to tip the headmaster five pounds when they left. Whether they paid their poll tax in gratitude or relief at escaping, it must have brought him in a tidy sum. But Eton had more serious failings, and by the middle of the century there were 'fearful stories of drunkenness & people do not scruple to name two of the masters as not being free from that vice'. It was one that was more likely to worry parents than boys, who for the most part seem to have taken the rough with the smooth, at school as at home. Lord Berners' description of his years at Eton, though he was probably exceptionally aware of the aesthetic appeal of the place, gives a good idea of what the school did – and did not do – for one boy:

> Eton was for me an Alma Mater beloved for her beauty more than for any other quality, and the memory of it was the most valuable of her gifts.
>
> In so far as my education was concerned, I had learned nothing, less than nothing, a minus quantity. I had lost what little knowledge I had of foreign languages. In history, geography and science I had been confused rather than instructed. I left Eton with a distaste for the Classics and, what was more serious, a distaste for work itself.

Looking back over his years at Eton, he decided like many others that he did not regret having been there. He left it 'as Antony left Cleopatra, with more love than benediction'.

The *Zeitgeist* of any century comes from the interaction of accepted traditions and rebellious reaction. And both traditions and rebels were strong at that time – mainly in religious, political and social contexts. Among the earliest of the religious rebels – though perhaps it would be fairer to call them questioners than rebels – were the Quaker Gurneys. The children were brought up within the strict, homespun, puritanical, 'good works' tradition of Friends, but they avoided the narrowness that this sometimes has. John Gurney and his guests discussed new ideas both with and in front of his children. They talked about the French Revolution and its aims, and how far these had been achieved; and of course they talked about religion. All the children kept a daily journal, and when she was thirteen Richenda Gurney wrote in hers: 'At this time I do not believe in Christ' – a sentence whose first three words show as much maturity as the rest show honesty. The young Gurneys mixed freely with children of other classes and other religions, though for some reason their father discouraged their friendship with a Unitarian family.

A different kind of religious rebellion turned up in the Stanley family when their eldest son Henry, in his mid-teens, became an enthusiastic

Arabist, working away for hours at Arabic grammar in order to read
Oriental Languages at Cambridge. There was nothing in his background or his childhood circumstances to turn him in that direction, but
eventually he caused quite a stir in his family and his class, as has been
seen, by becoming a Muslim and travelling in the East in Turkish dress.
The Gurneys and Henry Stanley were conscientious, thinking non-
conformists, who made their own way to the independent religious
stands they eventually took. There is a characteristic story of another
free-thinker who suffered for his sincerity at a very early age and later
was to go to prison for it. Bertrand Russell was told by his governess that
people who did not believe in Father Christmas did not get any
Christmas presents. Unable either to stretch his faith as far as that or to
pretend to a belief he did not feel, he burst into tears. Edith Sitwell was
also an infant rebel. When she was eleven she used to be 'kept in' every
Saturday afternoon because she would not recite by heart 'Casabianca',
the poem which told how 'The boy stood on the burning deck'. She had
a conscientious objection to doing this because, she said, she thought the
boy was idiotic not to move when the battle was raging all round him.
It evidently never occurred to her that perhaps it was equally idiotic
of her to lose all those Saturday afternoons for a rather similar
reason.

The future Lady Gregory was a political rebel at the same age. Her
Irish home was bare of books, which she had to borrow from the village
schoolmaster, and the family were not encouraged to discuss things
with their parents or each other. She was the only one of the sixteen
children who wanted to buy a Fenian pamphlet or a book of Irish
ballads, paying for these with the precious sixpence she had earned by
repeating her Bible passage without a slip. Another young political
rebel was 'brought up a Tory' though she always felt herself to be a
radical. When she was a child Lady Durham could never bear, she said,
to think of the division between the classes, and she declared that she
loved working men because they were 'so much better than we are'. The
clergyman who was preparing her for confirmation gave her a useful
lesson in integrity. One day when he came to teach her he saw on the
table a novel that her French governess was reading. French novels were
condemned at sight by many Victorian moralists who had never
attempted to read any of them. 'My dear child,' the clergyman said, 'you
don't read these things, do you?' Before she had time to answer he told
her not to make a promise 'for fear you should not keep it, but don't do it

unless you are obliged'. The advice fell on fruitful soil. 'And I never have', Lady Durham could say, many years later.

Today it is hard to imagine how the inequalities of nineteenth-century life could have been so complacently accepted by the privileged classes. Often it was these that first awoke children's doubts, leading them on to question other accepted conventions. Why were there some children they could play with, and others who were out of bounds? Lord William Russell and his wife were among the few aristocratic parents who liked their children to make friends outside their class, and their son Odo appreciated and was grateful for this when the family were in Carlsbad and he mixed with the tradespeople there. Perhaps it was easier to have a broader view of society from a Continental vantage-point. Lady Ottoline Morrell remembered that it was the sudden move to Welbeck Abbey, when life became very different for her, that made her realize what frivolously futile lives many upper-class women led.

Other children were less segregated because their parents had positively democratic attitudes. The third Earl Stanhope was an enthusiastic champion of the French Revolution – he signed his letters 'Your sincere and faithful Fellow-Citizen' – and he was delighted when his sixteen-year-old daughter became engaged to a commoner, a surgeon in Sevenoaks, near the Stanhope home at Chevening. 'Lucy is soon going to be married to a most worthy young man of her own chusing', he wrote to a friend. 'Her mind is liberal, and she despises Rank and *Aristocracy* as much as I do. I have seen much both here and abroad, of the middling classes; and I have observed, by far, more happiness there, as well as virtue, than amongst those Ranks of Men who insolently term themselves their *betters*.'

Lord Stanhope had realized that if Lucy's mind was to be 'liberal' by the time she was sixteen and of an age to choose a husband, she must be spared the socially segregated childhood of most of her class. The point was also taken by William Wilberforce, the anti-slavery pioneer, who is said to have refused a peerage so as not to deprive his children of 'the company of gentlemen, *les familles de commerce*, etc.'.

Across the centuries, words like Lord Stanhope's and William Wilberforce's help to fill the gaps on a page of social history that it is not altogether easy to research. It is not much use comparing the lives of the children of the great nineteenth-century country houses with those from similar or different backgrounds today. There is no putting the clock back – and not many would want to do if they could. But it can perhaps be interesting – even enjoyable, it may be hoped – to hear about lives, circumstances and ideas so different from those that were to come. Even, in Lewis Carroll's words:

> – though the shadow of a sigh
> May tremble through the story,
> For 'happy summer days' gone by,
> And vanish'd summer glory.

PART TWO

15

The Howards
at Naworth and
Castle Howard

The remarkable pattern and tempo of the Howards' family life during the second half of the nineteenth century was almost entirely due to the destructive philanthropist who was married to George Howard. Like Bertrand Russell's mother, Rosalind Howard was a daughter of that other doughty matriarch, Lady Stanley of Alderley. In 1889 George became the ninth Earl of Carlisle. Both were very young when they married in 1864, and they loved each other with a devotion that seems to have survived even the incompatibility which in the end made it impossible for them to live under the same roof. It was Rosalind's intransigence that drove her sons to leave home and helped to bring five out of the six to an early death.

Rosalind's life has been said to have paralleled the transition from government by the aristocratic, land-owning families to the first real practice of democracy in this country. Her Stanley background gave her a progressive Liberal springboard, and from this she took a header into the deep end of radical politics, women's emancipation and the temperance movement. She was one of those characters it is more enjoyable to read about than to live with, and she can be seen – close-up and life-size, but comfortably tamed by print – in the affectionate but not uncritical biography of her by her daughter Dorothy Henley. Rosalind was intelligent, well educated, widely read and, for a girl of her class and time, unusually aware of the social problems of the day. She had had the advantage of meeting and hearing the conversation of distinguished people in her parents' home, and she was not afraid to disagree with them. While still in her teens, she did not hesitate to tell Dr Benjamin Jowett, the redoubtable Master of Balliol, that he really ought to read *The Arabian Nights*.

The first twenty years of the Howards' marriage were happy enough. Rosalind gave birth to eleven children, and they lived mostly at Naworth Castle, the family home in Cumberland, then the property of George Howard's uncle, and recently restored after a disastrous fire. At that time the children adored their mother unquestioningly. Mary, the eldest, put their feelings into words when she wrote a story for Rosalind's birthday and presented it to her from her children, 'whose life she makes, by her endlessly loving thought, for us one long bright festa'. The festa was idyllically free and adventurous, in spectacularly wild and beautiful surroundings. They had very few rules or vetoes. They explored on foot or on their ponies wherever they wanted to go, and climbed and raced to their hearts' content over the castle rooftops. Another freedom they were allowed sounds less adventurous, but at that time it was both valuable and unusual. They were allowed to visit any house on the vast estate, and cottagers and tenants always gave them a great welcome. Dorothy Henley was the second youngest daughter, and she tells how she and her brother used to visit even those 'farmers who were famous tipplers' – it was broad-minded of Rosalind, with her temperance ideas, to allow this – and would be treated by their wives to plate-cake and girdle-cake. Dorothy and Michael called at the home farms, went to agricultural sales and auctions, and got up before six o'clock in summer to learn how to milk and to make butter in the old barrel churns. Michael learned shepherding and Dorothy was taught to plough, and proudly took her place in the Naworth team at a ploughing-match which lasted from first light to dusk.

It was a happy time, and Dorothy seldom remembered the younger children getting into trouble. Their mother had her own ploys and did not see much of them, leaving it to one of the older sisters to see the little ones to bed, and to her husband to read aloud to them. She did go with them on their magnificent picnics and expeditions – sometimes to very far-off places. They usually went by wagonette, a four-wheeled carriage, either open or with a cover that could be taken off, with five or six seats facing each other on either side, and usually two of the youngest children perched high up on the box with the coachman. If they were too many for the wagonette, extra dog-carts were brought along. The children enjoyed getting off and walking when they went up or down a hill.

At both homes the family had a wide choice of games and sports. At Castle Howard, in Yorkshire, their eighteenth-century *palazzo*,

Between 1865 and 1884 eleven children were born to George and Rosalind Howard, seen here with their daughter Bessie.

there were regattas on the lake, with Balliol undergraduates at the oars; there were also two-day cricket-matches, punctuated by luncheon for the teams in the Grecian Hall, and teas on long tables under the walnut trees alongside the pitch. There were tennis courts, croquet lawns and a bowling-green. Both houses had a squash court, and Castle Howard had a gymnasium as well as good rowing-boats; at Naworth there was a challengingly high 'giant's stride' – a tall pole with ropes hanging from its revolving top – as well as a man-size see-saw.

One game was too dangerous, and was stopped by George Howard. Dorothy told how a rope was tied to two trees on opposite sides of a steep valley at Naworth, and a shorter rope was tied round the middle of this, 'with a stirrup at its free end and a tailpiece to catch it by. The player swung across the wide chasm, and, by a faulty jump, or take-off, could be left in mid-air at a great height'. There was also archery – on one occasion the children nearly killed a visitor – and they staged spectacular roof-battles high up over the castle. They also had hose-battles, which involved plugging hoses into the hydrants below two of the towers and pulling these out to their full length before turning the water on at full cock. After that the everyday, homelier games they played sound rather tame. These included chess, old maid, piquet, shuvette, and commerce, a card-game for up to twenty players of all ages, which was usually played for money but, because Rosalind disapproved of gambling, the Howards played it for presents instead.

The family enjoyed the magnificent parties that were given at Naworth. Although these began early in the evening and went on till four or five the next morning, the children were allowed to stay up till the guests were leaving. They joined in the sumptuous supper, danced with any partners who offered themselves, and when they could no longer keep their eyes open they took a nap on a sofa in the midst of the revels. Other 'fun' occasions which must also have been useful social training were the annual Rent Dinners for the tenants. These took place in the vast hall at Naworth, and the children were told to mix with the guests, play their parts as hosts, and get into conversation with everyone they came across. Dorothy Henley tells of an entertaining dialogue on one of these occasions between herself, aged nine, and Mr Burtholme, the head woodman. The little girl did her best. 'Is the wheat crop good?' she inquired valiantly. 'Well, to tell truth,' the woodman answered with a smile, 'there isn't much on't round here.' After that, she said, they became fast friends.

George Howard's drawing of himself, playing 'Race' with four of his sons.

The after-dinner speeches were boring for the children, but they made up for such tedious moments in the days which followed, when they blew soap-bubbles for days on end with the unused clay pipes that had been provided on the dinner-table. At meals, once again, Rosalind Howard insisted on this courtesy of attempting to find some common ground for conversation. Dorothy remembered how later, at her first grown-up dinner-parties, if for a moment she found herself tongue-tied she would hear a sharp whisper from her mother: '*Parle donc, pourquoi ne parles-tu pas?*'

Christmas at Naworth was a jamboree for the local schoolchildren as well as for the family. The tree, over twenty feet high, called for the combined muscle of the six Howard boys and five others from nearby Lanercost vicarage. Parents, children, maids, governesses, the vicar's wife and the coachman's wife were all enlisted to make huge paper-chains and to fix dozens of candles on the branches of the tree. Before the great day the waits, as well as choirs from both church and chapel, trudged up to the Castle to sing and to play handbell tunes in the courtyard. Dorothy remembered seeing them sometimes in moonlight, sometimes in snow, with lamps and candles shining out through the great uncurtained windows. Then the singers and ringers came in to supper at the long dining-table down the centre of the flagged, uncarpeted floor of the great hall. Round the supper party, tapestries and family portraits hung on the old stone walls; alongside stood fifteenth-century heraldic beasts, six feet high, and suits of armour which on quieter occasions the Howard boys enjoyed putting on and wearing for a fight. Meanwhile coals blazed away in the fireplace, which was so large that the children would look up the chimney to see the clouds or the stars in the sky above.

Before Christmas was over, the tree was lit two or three times so that children from all the local schools could come and enjoy it; afterwards they had a festive tea in the billiard-room, with the young Howards again joining them and doing the honours. At Christmas the family and their friends also staged some splendid plays. One of these was seen by four hundred children and grown-ups. There were printed programmes, a roomy stage was built on the dais of the hall, and seats were ramped so that even the smallest members of the audience could see the actors. The plays were among the few activities which Rosalind did not initiate and guide; her talents lay elsewhere, and it was George Howard who directed them brilliantly. He and the local vicar, both

The Howard family and Italian neighbours with the Christmas tree on the Riviera, in 1878 – as festive an occasion as when Christmas was spent at home. A drawing by George Howard.

good at acting, outlined the story – Aladdin and Beauty and the Beast were among the subjects they chose – and they rehearsed enthusiastically, helped by any tutor who was interested, and with the children of about five nearby families as the cast. Performances were given on three nights so that all the local schoolchildren could come to the Castle – mainly in farm wagons, which must have added to the excitement – and see the play before tucking in to the splendid tea in the billiard-room.

So what was it that turned so much affection, splendour and *joie de vivre* to bitterness and animosity? The main cause, it seems, was Rosalind's fanaticism. She was fanatical about politics (she was a Liberal), about drink (she was a teetotaller whose children joined her when she 'took the pledge' in 1881), about sex, health and religion. She held to her principles unwaveringly and intransigently, and imprinted them on her children with missionary zeal. One of her sermons thundered on for six hours without a pause. Dorothy tells how on another occasion one of the girls, in her early teens, mentioned to her mother that she enjoyed using the prerogative of land-owners through whose estates the railway lines had been driven, by stopping the express so that she could get out at Naworth station. Privilege was one of Rosalind's hobby-horses, and the subject launched her on a harangue, which lasted a whole afternoon, about social 'wrongs' ranging from privilege to prostitution. Her daughter had never before heard of prostitution, and she was horrified by all the startling information which her mother hurled at her.

At this distance, Rosalind sounds impossibly intolerant and humourless, as well as curiously totalitarian for one who claimed to be a Liberal. Her children grew accustomed to her unpredictability. Dorothy was once caught dropping a wet sponge on the head of a pantry-boy who was about her age. This caused her mother to lecture her about the evils of flirtation – hardly likely to be relevant – until her daughter fainted. But that was another of Rosalind's *bêtes noires*. When Dorothy was accused of flirting with some undergraduates the children had met on a seaside holiday, retribution was awaiting her when she got home. She and her governess were subjected to a week of what her mother called '*lits de justice*' – the name of the famous judgement thrones of the French kings – while Rosalind lectured them in turn behind the locked door of the Tapestry Room. One of the undergraduates innocently added fuel to the flames by sending Dorothy a giant box of expensive chocolates from Buzzards, then the favourite source of luxury sweets and cakes. Rosalind ordered Dorothy to send them back, but she refused, and it is good to hear that she won the day, and that the chocolates were enjoyed by all who were then in the schoolroom.

It is difficult now to imagine how a woman who had had eleven children could be so obsessional about sex. Her attitude could not have been less helpful to her daughters, as she just thundered at them and explained nothing. Explanations were left in the not very well qualified hands of governesses, who were often foreigners and consequently not well provided with the right vocabulary for such delicate matters. One young woman from Italy was quite unequal to the task. When menstruation called for something in the way of a biology lesson, she could not manage anything more than sympathy. '*Poveretta!*' she giggled, '*poveretta!*' Another Howard daughter was tortured by anxiety about sex. Once when they were travelling in a train in France, she and her governess had to share their *wagon-lit* carriage with a male passenger. What would happen? the poor girl longed to discover. Did it mean that she might 'get a baby'? But of course the Howard sons-in-law were not the only nineteenth-century husbands whose brides had a lot to learn.

On other subjects their mother's teaching was less dogmatic, and sometimes positively progressive. She roused the children's sympathy and anger at the plight of the evicted Irish peasants and the miners who went on strike so effectively that Dorothy, at least, gave them all her pocket-money. The younger children had a practical training in social work by doing jobs that were useful to their mother. Dorothy and Michael were sent out on foot or on their ponies, or even driving themselves (without any adult) in the dog-cart, to visit families their mother was concerned about, and to see whether the houses were clean and tidy. They took blankets, an old suit of their father's, some tea, or an order for milk from the grocer. Later they would be sent back to see if the gifts had ended up in the pawn-shop. In the end Michael refused to go on these errands, so his sister went alone. She came to enjoy the affectionate contacts with people in such different circumstances, hearing from grannies and grandfathers about the old beliefs and customs of their young days, and drinking numberless cups of tea.

Sometimes Rosalind seems to have asked rather too much of her young daughter. Dorothy would go on her own to church, either driving herself like the farmers did, or else sitting in lonely state in the victoria, drawn by a pair of coach-horses and with a liveried coachman on the box. One occasion when she had to represent her mother was the first funeral she had ever been to. She had never seen anyone dead before, and was taken in to the front parlour where an old cottage-woman lay in her open coffin. She was a little unnerved when they asked her to stroke the old woman's cold face, but she managed it and after that never minded when asked to do this.

Rosalind asked the children to read aloud to her, to copy out her accounts and estate reports, to type, rearrange pictures and furniture, order meals, and discuss farm and cottage plans. She made even more personal demands on them: as she grew older, she asked them for a helping push up stairs or hills, to massage all parts of her body, to wake up at night to fill a hot-water-bottle or give her as many as six different medicines she was taking at one time, and even to sleep in the same bed with her. They wrote letters for her, asking for money and holiday hospitality for children from the crowded Yorkshire industrial towns. Hundreds of these were welcomed into farms, cottages, vicarages and Castle Howard itself, where of course the family were called upon to make the visitors feel at home.

Most of this was easy to understand and accept. But religion was more confusingly presented to the young Howards. They were encouraged to think for themselves about this, as about politics, by listening to grown-up discussions which expressed a wide range of views. Their parents' attitudes alone were enough to stimulate inquiring minds: their father had begun as a free thinker and later became a unitarian, whereas their mother began as a convinced low churchwoman and later became a free thinker. Neither parent was indifferent to religion; they both went to church if they expected the preacher to be good, taking the children with them but letting them read fairy tales during the sermon if this proved beyond them. What did it all add up to? For Dorothy the result was that she lost her 'nursery religion' by the age of eleven, and from then was an agnostic.

The children were introduced to politics very young. When George stood for Parliament, Rosalind canvassed the local farmers and once claimed to have done this for thirteen hours in one day. Often she took a young child along with her. Characteristically, she was a pioneer who insisted on breast-feeding her babies, so at such times she paused from canvassing and retired to nurse her child at a nearby vicarage. She never seems to have thought that politics and small children were perhaps not suited for each other. When Dorothy was very young, she was taken to a crowded and noisy local meeting about Home Rule for Ireland, and she fell asleep in her chair on the platform. When she was fourteen she was proud and excited to be sent as a local delegate to the Women's Liberal Federation Council in London. By that age young Howards were used to being called upon to speak in public – often at local temperance meetings.

Because Rosalind's public engagements were based on both her homes, she and the children often commuted between the two. Dorothy, still in the schoolroom, would be sent from Cumberland to Yorkshire to stand in for her mother as hostess to a party of anti-quarians, or members of a political group, or a factory outing. But lessons were not interrupted for frivolous reasons, and the schoolroom was allowed very meagre holidays – only Saturday afternoons, Sundays, birthdays, Christmas and New Year's Day, apart from the great occasions when they all went off for whole days to Hexham, the moors, an agricultural show or a cricket match. There was no question of the children being pampered. Their food was plentiful but plain, and at every breakfast their governess carefully cut a boiled egg in two and gave half each to Dorothy and Michael. Until they were about twelve, when their pocket-money was stepped up to a shilling, they each had only twopence a week. (Later, their mother recognised that this had not been enough, and made up for it by giving them fifty pounds each.) The weekly twopence was doled out by Rosalind's secretary, and when he was busy he sometimes got as much as six weeks in arrears. But the children were taught never to ask for anything, so they waited wretchedly outside the library door, tossing up to decide who would go in and claim the money.

After the early years of acceptance and love, the children gradually saw that some of their mother's ideas and actions were questionable, but the girls still kept their affection for her, diplomatically directing discussions to impersonal subjects. The boys suffered far more disastrously from their upbringing. Their father had been unhappy at Eton, and so decided that it was better for boys to be educated at home by tutors. Two of his sons did go away to school, but the others learned languages from their sisters' governesses and had tutors for mathe-matics and science. Their mother loved them adoringly but she antagonised them all and drove them away from home. Only one boy was not damaged by growing up in this matriarchal environment; two of them were permanently crippled by it and became alcoholics; almost all

161

the boys refused to come home after they were grown-up; and all but one of the six died before their mother did.

To make matters worse, Rosalind chose hopeless tutors for her sons. They were usually second-rate schoolmasters or recent Oxbridge graduates. One wretched man had a Welsh accent and the boys imitated and ragged him endlessly, setting booby-traps, firing off chemical stinks, and raising hell in the schoolroom. Another unfortunate man came from a town elementary school, and had a plebeian voice and manners. Experience with a large group of working-class ten-year-olds did not help him with the Howard boys, and his lessons often ended in fisticuffs, and once brought him to table with a bandaged head. At one point one of Her Majesty's Inspectors came to test them. His verdict was that they had no mastery of 'the three R's' – reading, writing and arithmetic – but were quite well grounded in languages, literature, chemistry and astronomy. Somehow the system worked better for the girls, who liked their governesses – though one Fräulein had recourse to the classic chastisement of knuckle-rapping with her ruler.

The parental split, when it came, tore the family up by its roots. In spite of deep affection, Rosalind had irreconcilable political disagreements with George – and eventually with some of her sons too – on such burning issues of the day as the Boer War and Irish Home Rule. She felt deeply and intolerantly, lost her temper quickly, and made the fatal mistake of dominating and repressing others. When there was a flare-up, Rosalind sometimes turned her sons out of the house without considering that perhaps they might be too proud to return.

Less has been written about George Howard than about his wife, but he sounds a charming man, devoted to his children, free of any snobbery or pretentiousness, interested mainly in art and literature, and friendly with many writers and painters. He took Dorothy, when she was in London, to see Watts and the Holman Hunts, and went with Michael and her to Hampton Court and the Tower of London. It must have been an additional thrill for the children to travel by the Underground, and third-class at that. This meant sitting in a 'Smoking' compartment on wooden benches, and the atmosphere was sulphurous and choking. Dorothy was sick all over the carriage, and it was then suggested to their father that his journeys with the children should be a little less spartan.

When George and Rosalind Howard separated, he left her both homes to live in though he visited them from time to time – usually to paint or to fish. Of course it was helpful that their homes happened to be

George Howard and his six sons. Rosalind Howard's intransigence drove them all away, and was a main reason for bringing five of the boys to an early death.

vast castles, big enough to allow each a completely separate territory, and that there was a large house for them all in London too. Dorothy remembered occasions when, though both parents were under the same roof, they communicated by letter, often using her as their postman and go-between. When they parted they agreed that George would be responsible for the oldest children (apart from two daughters who were already married), leaving the younger ones with their mother. The older girls tried to bridge the rift between Rosalind and her husband and sons, but she remained intransigent. Her eldest son wanted his two youngest sisters to be bridesmaids at his wedding, and the children begged to be allowed this. But there was not a chance of it. The girls were not even allowed to be present, and their mother stayed away too.

It is a tragic story, best summed up, perhaps, by Rosalind's mother, old Lady Stanley of Alderley, and the rest of her family. Watching the whole Aeschylean drama rumble on its relentless way, they all agreed that Rosalind Howard, with her virtue and her determination, 'was enough to drive anyone to vice or drink'.

16

The Cecils at Hatfield

In 1868 Robert Cecil succeeded his father as third Marquess of Salisbury, and it was his family of five sons and two daughters whose childhood makes such interesting reading today, and who all grew up to be such outstanding and distinguished individuals. They have been fully described elewshere, but no book about childhood in the great nineteenth-century country houses can fail to include them. The Salisbury parents met their children on an entirely level footing, questioning and discussing everything (with slight reservations about the all-important subject of religion) with them. They seem to have been never too busy for endless conversations. 'My father always treats me as if I were an ambassador,' said one of his sons, 'and I do like it.' Lord Salisbury could also modulate into a lighter key, and would let the boys tug him – weighing eighteen stone and enthroned on a fur rug – up and down the long Hatfield Gallery. Later, in the years which included his terms of office as Foreign Secretary and Prime Minister, he enjoyed a race down the same Gallery with his young grandchildren.

Lady Salisbury was just as close to her children – if perhaps less boisterously. It was she who read to them, prepared them for confirmation, and guided their religious education. (Every day at Hatfield began with prayers in the Chapel for family and staff, and every Sunday evening there was a service there with Communion.) The value of her teaching can perhaps be judged by the fact that to all seven children – one of them became a bishop – their religion remained throughout their lives all-important.

It might be said that ideas were bread-and-butter to the young Cecils. They had generous helpings of conversation at breakfast, when there were letters and newspapers by way of appetizers for political and other discussions; and these went on throughout the day, until on their several ways to bed the family were still talking, at the foot of the stairs or at their bedroom doors. The children were unusually free, both physically and intellectually. They could climb to dizzy heights over the Hatfield roofs, skate hair-raisingly on the ice, try out the fire-arms in the Armoury, and gallop their ponies at breakneck speed through the park. They were equally free to read anything that took their fancy in the library, to be unpunctual, badly dressed or downright dirty at meals, and to disagree with their parents' eminent friends. There are several versions of a famous story of the encounter between the five-year-old Hugh Cecil and Gladstone, who was visiting Hatfield. One of the earliest sets the scene in Gladstone's room, where he was left to rest alone after tea. Young Hugh went in and started pummelling the politician who he knew was his father's opponent. 'You're a very bad man', he told him. 'How can I be a bad man when I am your father's friend?' Gladstone asked him. But the boy assured him that his father shared his opinion. And that was not all. 'My father is going to cut off your head with a great big sword,' he added.

Some humorous and affectionate letters to their parents, written by the young children, are still in the Hatfield archives. All (except one sister) had comic nicknames, and a letter in a very juvenile fist from Hugh Cecil, known by his family as Linky, ends on a somewhat prophetic note: 'P.S. If I am a great man 300 years hence my letters signed L. Linkey will be immensely valuable.' It was, of course, the custom of the day to sign easy, informal letters 'Your affec. son' (or daughter). There was certainly no lack of affection on either side. 'Dearest lovely Mama (as I am nearly 14)', a letter from Robert Cecil begins; Edward Cecil, known as 'Nigs', writing from school, starts several in the same way: 'Dear dear dearest Mama'; while one from William, the future Bishop of Exeter, who was known as 'Fish' by way of an abbreviation for 'Queer Fish', begins: 'Most beloved Mother', and goes on to add:

PS I am happy
NB But I still love you.

Maud, the eldest daughter, is equally loving in rather a different way: 'Well my dear old Mama,' she starts one letter, 'I want you to give me a box of tools, especially the gluepot and a sovering [sic], if you don't like to give me the Sovering give me a bottle of scent instead.'

Lord and Lady Salisbury clearly treasured their children's letters, keeping them all, from the earliest scraps and drawings to a more sophisticated note, written by Edward Cecil when he was fifteen: 'Dear Papa,

Hatfield House,
Hatfield,
Herts.

my Dear Mama i ought to have put a capital letter at the beginning. Nigs is quite well i have been to church.

your affectionate fish

An early letter to his mother from William Cecil (known to his family as 'Fish'), the future Bishop of Exeter.

I write as a younger son always ought to write to his father for money unless you wish me to be detained here for attempting to fly from my creditors.' Lord Salisbury's answer is not in the archives, but somehow it seems unlikely that he left his son to the tender mercies of the duns.

The children's letters also have a lot to tell about how they spent their time. They rode, went for long walks, played tennis, skated, hunted rabbits and rats, played chess, read books and newspapers and comics, acted charades, made scrapbooks, flew kites, and gardened. An early letter, dictated at a time when the future Bishop of Exeter was not up to writing for himself though he managed to sign himself 'Fish', told his mother that he was building a lovely shop, up in the stables, but he had not learned his hymn. Gwendolen, writing from Hatfield when she was eight, tells her mother exactly what is going on. 'We four older ones Maud me Jem and Fish, played at robers this afternoon in the shrubery and we had pistols and shot caps out of them. . .and tell Papa that we have not got to the rule of three to his great disgust.' After this, formality breaks in and the letter changes key to end 'Believe me, Your most affectionate. . .'

It is always interesting to see what presents children ask for – even if they do not always get what they want. One of the Cecil girls asked for a dinner set and a work-box with a crochet-needle in it. Maud waited impatiently for a new saddle and bridle, while the boys wanted gunpowder, a whip and a box of marbles. Gwennie gave Bob her trowel, someone else had a pack of cards, and there were presents of a knife, some inspiringly decorated writing-paper (with a gay pictorial border) and, for each of the girls, a Bible. The Cecils were often ill (though they all lived to great ages) and the letters tell of coughs, sore throats, bad backs and shoulders, and rheumatism. There was anxiety about their grandparents' health as well. The future fourth Marquess, in his early teens, wrote to his mother about his grandmother. 'I think she is much better,' he told her, 'because I prayed to God to make her well.' But the children had to learn that prayers were sometimes not granted. Their grandmother died, and the letters tell how the older children reacted. 'Granny will be in a happier land,' Robert wrote trustingly. 'God will make her happy for ever.' Gwendolen had the same faith. 'Granny has gone to a much happier place than this,' she wrote; there she would see her dead husband and son again.

Because of his own unhappy schooldays Lord Salisbury decided that his sons should be educated at home by tutors until they were ready for

Eton. There was, of course, no question of the girls going away to school. Up to a point the system worked well. The children all learned to think and question for themselves, to read omnivorously, to be truthful, charitable and unmaterialistic, and to take part confidently in well-informed adult conversation. They were particularly – if perhaps rather one-sidedly – well grounded in religion and politics. There is a story of Linky, the future Baron Quickswood, declaring at the age of six: 'My Nana is I am afraid a Socinian: I myself was for long not quite orthodox.' Today that sounds very priggish, but even a long-distance acquaintance with the young Cecils is enough to establish that the youthful theologian was certainly pulling his own leg.

Inevitably, the Cecil boys were unprepared for the rigours of Eton. They had never played cricket or football, and had not learned to be punctual, to obey orders or to keep their inquiries on narrow, prescribed lines. No wonder they did not enjoy school much. Lord Salisbury told each of his sons that if ever he found himself likely to get a flogging he was to take the next train for home. It was an attitude to school and schoolmasters that went on into this century. Lord David Cecil was at Eton during the first World War, and his father commiserated with him about one of the beaks. 'It must be trying for you', he said, 'to spend much of your time with such an inferior man.'

Visitors to Hatfield were sometimes startled to hear young children disagreeing and even contradicting their parents' distinguished friends. It is said that a foreign girl who was staying in the house, hearing the children so often call their father a 'goose', imagined it must be an affectionate pet-name. It certainly did not mean that they had no respect for him. His daughter (who was also to be his biographer) described how their father was 'clearly so miserable if he thought any of us were not doing our best that it was too uncomfortable to go on'. The picture becomes three-dimensional when it is added to Lady Salisbury's description of her husband 'sitting as usual, humble and silent among his sons'.

Another view of the Cecils in the 1880s comes from the account published in France by Dr Coppini, a French tutor. Lady Salisbury wanted someone who could take his place like a friend or a guest at the family dinner table, and would speak French with her children. Being a convinced republican as well as a non-practising Roman Catholic, Coppini had his doubts; but he was asked to turn up in September 1883 at the family's holiday house near Dieppe. His first meeting with

William Cecil, then sixteen, encouraged him. The boy saw that his tutor was reading a book about Sir Robert Peel. 'What a man!' said the tutor, admiringly. 'I detest him,' answered William Cecil. 'He's a traitor.' Coppini gazed at him in amazement. 'I am a Conservative,' said the boy, 'and you are a Liberal.' 'Yes.' 'We'll get on all right nevertheless. You'll see.' And they did. It was a typically Cecilian exchange.

Another 'outsider' who was warmly welcomed into the family and has left vivid descriptions of it is the Rev. C. L. Dodgson, better known as Lewis Carroll, the author of *Alice in Wonderland*. He was introduced to Lord Salisbury at Oxford in 1870, at the time of his installation as Chancellor of the University; being a keen pioneer amateur photographer, he was delighted to be allowed to photograph the new Chancellor with his two sons as his train-bearers. He showed the four eldest Cecil children the first of the illustrations for *Alice through the Looking-Glass*, took some more pictures of them, and began a lasting friendship with them and their parents. Carroll, a forty-year-old don who was ordained but prevented by shyness and a stammer from officiating as a priest, was a strange genius of unique wit and imagination, whose two passions were mathematics and little girls. As he put it himself, he was 'fond of children (except boys)'. He is said to have been attracted to little girls by their looks rather than their brains, but his stories and jokes for children make heavy demands – at least by present standards – on their general knowledge and quickness of wit. The two delightful Cecil girls were certainly not beauties: they later came to be known as the Salisbury Plains. It seems that little girls were Carroll's only sexual pleasure, and that this was innocent enough. At that time Freud was still a schoolboy, and the girls, their parents and their entertainer-cum-photographer seem to have been unworried by any *arrière-pensées*, conscious or unconscious. He liked to photograph his nymphets either naked or wearing as little as possible, always kissed them and – it is not surprising to learn – preferred them to visit him unchaperoned. Just as some flowers instinctively attract the insects they need, Carroll found his own way of providing himself with a steady stream of little girl companions: he made himself endlessly interesting and amusing to them.

Carroll's diaries tell of frequent meetings with the young Cecils at Hatfield and in London. They enjoyed his famous wire-puzzles, card tricks and a game of his called Arithmetical Croquet, and for them he began composing verse-riddles and his 'Puzzles from Wonderland'. He

Lady Maud & Lady Gwendolen
1864

The 'Salisbury Plains' in 1864: Maud (born 1858) and Gwendolen (born 1860).

also usefully filled a gap in the girls' education. Their parents had no appreciation of the fine arts; as Lord Salisbury himself put it: 'Hatfield is Gaza, the capital of Philistia.' So Carroll took the girls to the Royal Academy, to the theatre to see Ellen Terry play Portia, and to concerts. But of course he was in demand most as a story-teller. On New Year's Eve, 1871, he arrived at Hatfield and found a large party in the great Gallery, playing charades. (The word was 'Chance-sell-law'.) After that, Carroll told them his story about pixies, and a Russian tale about a blacksmith and a hobgoblin. During his next two days at Hatfield he thought out a new chapter of *Sylvie and Bruno*, and told it to the same appreciative audience in the Gallery. A note in his diary that day reminded him to write the chapter out before he forgot it. Elveston, in *Sylvie and Bruno*, is almost certainly based on Hatfield, the Earl on Lord Salisbury, and Lady Muriel on one of the Cecil girls; most of the chapters were first told on Carroll's visits to Hatfield. It was not until the 1875 New Year's Eve party, when there was a ball for some hundred and fifty children, that Carroll at last jibbed at accepting his 'usual role of story-teller. . .and so (I hope) broke the rule of being always expected to do it'. His visits to the family continued, so it seems he was forgiven. An unusual criticism of Carroll at Hatfield came from Princess Alice, later Countess of Athlone, who remembered him there when she was a child. 'He was always making grown-up jokes to us,' she grumbled, 'and we thought him awfully silly.'

Another eminent visitor was Lord Salisbury's political opponent, Disraeli, who enjoyed a stroll up and down the Gallery, talking to one of the girls. The job of helping to entertain visitors was one the children took in their stride. They guided them on tours of the house and grounds, discoursing learnedly on family heirlooms or the latest Parliamentary argy-bargy. An elderly 'crocodile' would be seen, conscripted to play follow-my-leader up and down stairs, and along endless floors and passages; one account tells of distinguished guests sitting on the floor of the Gallery, puffing away at a feather which had to be blown across a sheet.

On other occasions informality was out of the question. Blanche Balfour, a young great-niece of Lord Salisbury, was present at one splendid Hatfield garden party which was attended by Queen Victoria in her old age. Lady Salisbury presented the little girl to the Queen, helpfully pressing her to a curtsey with a heavy hand on her shoulder. Blanche had another splendid recollection of bowling along with the

The photograph that Lewis Carroll took in 1870 of Lord Salisbury in his robes as Chancellor of Oxford University, with his sons in their train-bearer's suits.

Salisburys in an open carriage drawn by four fine horses. On the near side rode two postilions in white buckskin breeches and cockaded hats; pale blue satin rosettes shone on their dark blue livery coats, matching those on the horses' ears. An equally elegant coachman and footman sat enthroned high on the box of the carriage, which was followed by two mounted grooms. Inside, the little girl, aged six, sat by her mother opposite the vast dignified figure of Lord Salisbury, sitting beside his wife. As the carriage clattered into the streets of Hertford, there were cheers from the crowded pavements, graciously acknowledged by Lord Salisbury. Blanche tried to copy his gesture of thanks, but was quickly called to order by her mother, who whispered that the cheers were for Uncle Robert, not for her. It was the 1886 General Election, and the Hatfield party were visiting Hertford to hear the poll declared.

A formal occasion which cropped up every year was the Tenants' Dinner. It was a genial, friendly celebration, and in the time of the third Marquess the toast to Lady Salisbury and her family was replied to by Hugh Cecil, who from an early age was a witty and confident speaker. Christmas, of course, was another festive time. A Salisbury daughter-in-law has described the Armoury, lit by candles, where local choir-boys sang carols. Lady Salisbury sat with her grandchildren round her knees and on the steps. The young Cecils blew trumpets and beat drums as presents were given to the servants, some of the outdoor staff and the children. From their early years they had been used to sharing festivities with people outside the family circle. One Hatfield letter from a very young child announces that 'On my birthday I am going to have the Workhouse children to tea, also the infant school'. Training began early.

Today the ultra-paternalist ideas they were reared on seem hundreds of light-years away. Even then, many of the Cecils' fellow-Tories found their attitude outdated, with its resistance to any extension of the franchise and its insistence that political power was best used by men of education and landed property. The children of the third Marquess all learned in childhood to feel and work for those who were less fortunate than themselves. They all grew up with sensitive social consciences, and were conspicuous in their support of what to them (but often to few others) seemed to be good causes. In their different ways they all made their mark in the world.

They had been taught to think for themselves and to ask questions.

And yet on those two most important subjects – religion and politics – they all came safely home to roost in the family nest. It is not a bad plan to end on a question-mark. Why was it that the Cecils, unlike such families as the Stanleys, the Howards and the Russells, never produced a child who became a Muslim, an atheist or a socialist?

17

The Russells
at Ravenscroft and
Pembroke Lodge

The nineteenth-century Russells, like the Cecils, were a political family – though on the opposite side of the House – which produced an eminent statesman who was twice Prime Minister, as well as, in the present century, a distinguished writer. Both families were based on their great homes near London, where they also had a house. But there the likeness ends. For various reasons the Victorian Russells had much less happy childhoods than their Cecil contemporaries, and these left lasting scars on many of them, bringing them in their later years unhappiness, loneliness and, in two cases, eventual suicide. The Russell children who are the subject of this chapter knew extremes of happiness and wretchedness.

Their parents were the Prime Minister's eldest son, Viscount Amberley, and his wife Kate who was, like Rosalind Howard, a daughter of Lord Stanley of Alderley. Theirs was a happy though tragically short marriage, and detailed accounts of their life with their children have been left by their sons Frank and Bertrand. Both were to succeed to the title of Earl Russell, and Bertrand was to become one of the most important philosophers and political thinkers of his time. During their early years the children could not have had a happier or more enlightened upbringing. Both parents were devoted to them and spent much of their days and nights in their company; they had exceptionally progressive ideas about education and social relations, gradually during their first ten years together coming to discard their inherited religion and taking their own positive stand as agnostics.

From 1870, when Frank was about five, they lived near Tintern, just north of the Severn estuary, and he remembered their time there as one of unconventional freedom which was very unusual at that date. He slept in a cot at the foot of his parents' double bed, and was passionately fond of his mother, who spent most of her mornings teaching her children. Then and later, there were also various governesses and tutors, and Frank described his wet-nurse, Mrs Lizzie Williams, as 'the most important member of the household'. Once again the Amberleys were ahead of their times in following what Frank later called their 'democratic principles', allowing Mrs Williams's two young children to play 'on terms of complete equality' with the young Russells.

Even today Frank's education seems enviably stimulating. At five he could read, and before he was eight he had got through – for his own enjoyment – all Scott's novels. Some full-blooded oaths rubbed off on him on the way, and he is said to have startled his parents and their friends by sudden exclamations of ''zounds' and ''sdeath' without having any idea of what the words meant. He read voraciously; nothing was forbidden. From the age of about seven, he used to go out picking wild flowers, and then fixed these on paper, carefully writing by each one its botanical and common names as well as its properties and habitat. So lessons and pleasures merged into each other, as they always should. He enjoyed helping to make a rockery and a garden, and in playful moments driving his younger sister around in a wheelbarrow and in a little goat-carriage. But above all he was fascinated by machinery, and was delighted by a little vertical steam-engine he was given on his seventh birthday, and by constructing – on his own – a miniature water-wheel. Real-life engineering was to be found not far away; he used to ride down on his pony to Murray's Iron Works at Tintern, where he could watch a rolling mill, worked by water power, and a general engineering shop which was driven by steam. Best of all, the boy in charge of the hand-wheel sometimes let him help to turn it. Nearer home, it was also a pleasure to watch the threshing-machine at its work.

The ethical grounding the Amberleys gave their children was original and unusual. Frank never remembered being taken to church, hearing of heavenly rewards and punishments, or 'having the name of God inflicted on me'. Nor was he ever made to do anything just because he was told to; reason was the basis of everything. Instead of urging him not to tell lies, his parents somehow managed to give him 'a dislike for the sort of people who told lies'. The system was put into practice – somewhat uncomfortably – on Frank's seventh birthday. All day long, he was told, he could do exactly as he liked, so off he trotted on his pony to the village and with his own pocket-money made a vast purchase of treacle from the grocer. He took it home and feasted on it – with the inevitable consequences. No words had been spoken, and the lesson had been learned – the hard way – that 'there are natural laws which cannot be disobeyed with impunity'.

It was not always quite so ideal. Frank was beaten for stealing apples from an orchard near his home, and another time his father whacked him with the rough side of a hair-brush on his bare skin. His relations later told him that he was at that time 'an unwashed, ill-bred, impertinent little child dressed in rags'. At about the time of the famous seventh birthday, he went with his father on a round of country-house visits, and letters from his father to his mother told of endless naughtiness: the boy was disobedient, called his father 'a beast', and went on doing this when he saw how it enraged him. When Lord Amberley spoke of giving him his 'calming medicine', Frank knew very well what would happen. 'I think you'd better not,' he said. 'It will only make me stupid.' It sounds as if he must have had quite a few doses already, to be so sure of its effect.

When Frank was six and his sister Rachel was three, Lady Amberley was looking for a governess, and the letter she wrote to one applicant describes the children in detail. Frank, she said, was very clever and forward, but had recently 'overworked' and had been ordered '*no lessons*' for two or perhaps three years. The girl was '3 and rather backward; she only knows her letters but talks German as well as English & cares for singing'. Frank slept in his mother's room; Rachel would sleep with the governess. They both got up at half past six, and spent much of their time with their parents or out-of-doors. Their mother liked them to be 'much alone & unwatched'. The governess was certainly not left in any doubt about her employer's wishes and her determination that these should be followed. 'I do not care what your religion is,' Lady Amberley wrote, 'but I like no one to speak to the children on that subject but myself.'

Homely practical jobs were also part of Frank's training. He carted away barrowfuls of dead leaves, and was paid a farthing for each load. The children made their own beds and folded their clothes at night. Their mother liked them to 'learn to be *useful & independent*. . .Work of all sorts is to be taught them as necessary and desirable'. At seven Frank was learning to darn, and 'did' all his mother's dusters. 'All this winter', she wrote, 'he has done the housemaid's work of my room & the nursery

Frank Russell with his sister Rachel. Four years later she and their mother died of diphtheria.

very thoroughly & I find it a very useful occupation for him. Soon he will learn cooking.'

In May 1872, three months after Lady Amberley wrote this, Bertrand Russell was born. (It is amusing to hear that he narrowly escaped being named Galahad; his family and friends always called him Bertie.) A year or so later, a talented but strange scientist called Robert Spalding was engaged as tutor to Frank. His lessons were certainly not boring. For years his pupil remembered the experiments he staged. He cut the heart from a freshly-killed salmon and watched it go on beating for a long time – for twenty-four hours, Frank later thought. He also cut the head off a wasp, and together they watched the insect go on cleaning, with its legs, the place where its head had been. Spalding was especially interested in the instincts of chickens, and noted how soon after hatching they managed to pick up crumbs and feed themselves. No one could accuse his employers of having discouraged his work. They allowed the chickens all over the house, and Spalding also had robins and a hive of bees in his own room. Nor was that all. The tutor was seriously ill with consumption and had only a few years to live. The Amberleys felt that because of this he should avoid having any children but should not be expected to forego the joys of sex. They found an odd solution to the problem by agreeing that Spalding should sleep with Lady Amberley. Bertrand Russell, describing this arrangement in his autobiography, commented coolly that he had 'no reason to believe that she derived any pleasure from this'. Like his brother, Bertie was a precocious child, but surely at less than two years old he was a little young to make that particular assessment.

Just after Bertie's second birthday, disaster struck the family. In May 1874, Frank had diphtheria. His mother devotedly nursed him through it, but she and his sister also caught it, and by the first week of July both were dead. Lord Amberley, heart-broken and with no further interest in life, died eighteen months later. The two boys were with him at the end. His last words were to his older son. 'My poor boy,' he said, 'now you are indeed an orphan.' Frank kept a diary, and his entry for that day reads: 'Father died in the morning. Went sliding in the afternoon.' Writing later about this, Frank argued – not altogether convincingly – that his reaction was less callous than it sounds. Either way, it was a time of upheaval for the two surviving children. Their father left instructions that Spalding and another agnostic should be their guardians, to protect them 'from the evils of a religious upbringing'. But the Russell grandparents – Earl and Countess Russell – having heard of their daughter-in-law's relationship with Spalding, were equally determined to save the boys from 'the clutches of intriguing infidels'. In the end, both were made wards in Chancery and were sent to live with their grandparents in their retirement at Pembroke Lodge in Richmond Park; Countess Russell, her brother and her son were to be the boys' guardians. Bertie's earliest clear recollection was of travelling there by train in February 1876, and being given tea in the servants' hall. They perched him on a tall stool, and he wondered why they were all so interested in him.

The ideas and atmosphere of Pembroke Lodge could hardly have been more different from those the boys had known. Bertie was probably too young to feel the whole impact of the contrast; it must have been far worse for Frank. He looked back on it as a 'nightmare atmosphere', full of rules and taboos. At home he had been allowed to wander and ride wherever he liked, and the children were encouraged to run around barefoot. At Pembroke Lodge he could never go outside the grounds, to the nearby village of Petersham, or to Richmond. His parents had given their children plenty of time to themselves, but his grandmother now arranged that his every minute was supervised. His only getaway was high up on the roofs of the house, or up the tallest trees into their topmost branches.

The servants were a great comfort to Frank. An old housekeeper gave him biscuits and Turkish delight, both contraband because sugar was thought to be bad for children; the butler let him help to frank letters for the post; he enjoyed watching the footman clean his scores of lamps; and his grandmother's lady's-maid sometimes let him use her sewing-machine. These joys must have been a great help in adapting to the unfamiliar, austere regime of Pembroke Lodge. It must have been a shock to be taken to church for the first time, and he also had to turn up at family prayers each morning, and be lectured on morals and behaviour. His parents had encouraged inquiries into every subject under the sun; Frank now found that his questions remained unanswered. Fridays and Sundays were 'At Home' days, when he had to put in an appearance with tidy clothes, clean hands, and well-brushed hair. Bertie was cherished as an angel child, to be safe-guarded from his brother's damaging influence, so they were seldom left alone together.

Their grandmother did try to amuse the boys. She wrote little plays,

with music, for them to act. One of her verses evokes the very smell of
that well-polished, dustless house:

> Little Frank Russell
> He is in a bustle
> And what shall poor Granny do do-oo!
> On her sofa he jumps
> Her piano he thumps
> Oh dear what a hulla-ba-loo!

There was not much chance of these lines charming the boy who had
always been absorbedly interested in machinery, and one of whose
dearest possessions, at the age of eight, was a little wooden printing-
press given to him by George Grote, the eminent historian.

He was one of many interesting visitors to Pembroke Lodge. Queen
Victoria was friendly with the Russells, and Frank remembered her
coming to tea in 1874, when he was presented to her as she sat 'in state at
her separate tea-table with her separate tea-pot'. Apart from such great
occasions, the day began with prayers for family and servants, with a
hymn, a lesson from the Bible, and a prayer read by Lady Russell. After
that came breakfast for all the family, followed by lessons till midday,
when Frank played outside, mostly on his own; during the afternoon he
went for a drive in the carriage with his grandmother, or else he walked,
either alone or with his aunt. Between the end of dinner and bed-time he
read aloud for half-an-hour. What he hated was the atmosphere of
constant disapproval and the endless questionings. What had he done?
Where had he been? Whom had he seen? At that time, he remembered,
he was 'pining for love, understanding and companionship, and
bubbling over with the exciting confidences of youth'. The chill of his
childhood marked him for life. 'I never entirely recovered my natural
freedom and frankness', he lamented.

Looking back later on his grandparents' ideas, Frank wrote them off
as 'doubts, fears and hesitations, reticences and suppressions, and a sort
of mournful Christian humility'. He was forbidden to read most of the
books in the house – especially, it is puzzling to hear, those of Captain
Marryat, which all boys loved – but he managed to find and enjoy some
forgotten volumes high on the top shelves of his schoolroom. In the
evenings he was made to read aloud – sometimes from the sermons of
Dean Farrar, sometimes (much more enjoyably for him) from
Shakespeare. His narrow-minded but certainly well-intentioned

grandmother would have been flabbergasted to hear how Frank looked back on her attempts to guide his youthful steps. 'When I think of the way in which slushy innocence was being continuously extolled and forced upon my independent mind,' he wrote, 'I think it is much to my credit that I did not plunge headlong into vicious excesses.'

Bertie, too young to remember the paradise they had lost, was less unhappy, particularly during his early years. Pembroke Lodge was in the middle of Richmond Park, surrounded by eleven acres of garden – mostly wild – with splendid trees to climb, fountains where the boys could bathe, summer-houses, an aviary, and a bowling-green. These provided a comforting escape-route for Bertie. He remembered later how, all by himself, he 'used to wander about in the garden, alternately collecting birds' eggs and meditating on the flight of time'. Snippets of grown-up conversation the boys heard were always about times long past – about his grandfather's visit to Napoleon on Elba, about his great-great-great-uncle defending Gibraltar during the American War of Independence, about Carlyle, Herbert Spencer, Darwin, Gladstone and other venerable friends of his grandparents. A visitor to the house at that time remembered Bertie as a 'solemn little boy in a blue velvet suit, with an equally solemn governess'. At tea there, Lady Russell 'always spoke in hushed tones, Lady Agatha always wore a white shawl and looked downtrodden, Rollo Russell never spoke at all.' No wonder she found the house an 'unsuitable place for children'.

Bertie's grandfather was more than twenty years older than his wife; she also had two step-granddaughters, as they had married when he was left a widower with a young family to bring up. He used to be wheeled round the garden at Pembroke Lodge in a bath chair, and also sat indoors browsing on a volume of Hansard. (Did it date from the years when he had taken part in the debates, or was it a recent one? It would be interesting to know.) Once when the old man was ill and the Russells rented a house at Broadstairs, Frank found life so unbearable that he twice ran away. It was after this, and after he had refused to promise not to make a third shot at a getaway, that he was sent off to school, where he found himself for the first time called Viscount Amberley, much to his 'surprise and indignation'.

During Bertie's first years at Pembroke Lodge his grandmother held the centre of his stage, and her love and care of him sparked off his warm affection in return. Only when he was fourteen did he recognize that she had the 'strict morality of a Victorian puritan', and that her ethical and

183

intellectual narrowness were more than he could bear. Two other relations lived in the house: his Uncle Rollo, who fascinated him with meteorological talk about the unusual sunsets and a blue moon that were seen in England after the 1883 Krakatoa eruption; and his Aunt Agatha, who tried to teach Bertie his colours when he was three, and also – unsuccessfully – to read. When he was six she taught him English constitutional history, interested him keenly, and he remembered her lessons all his life.

Like his brother, he found the servants more genial than any of his family. He liked the old housekeeper, and sat on the knee of a Scottish butler who read him newspaper reports of railway accidents. A French cook frightened him when he went into the kitchen to watch the meat turning and roasting on a spit; when the boy stole lumps out of the salt-box, the cook chased him with a carving-knife but – not surprisingly – never managed to slash him with it. Outside, he liked a lodge-keeper and his wife, who gave him two forbidden treats – baked apples and beer.

So on the whole Bertie looked back on his early childhood as a happy time. He liked the German and Swiss governesses who looked after him and taught him to speak German almost as easily as English. Even so, his best moments were spent on his own, out-of-doors, enjoying flowers, trees and nests, sunsets, wind and lightning. His was a lonely happiness. He enjoyed the books – chiefly those of Maria Edgeworth to start with – which his grandmother read aloud to him, but she was of course a strict censor. One story she said was 'not very nice' so she would not read it. She might have known that nothing could be a more effective apéritif, and he read the whole story, a sentence at a time, each time he brought the book from the shelf to Lady Russell. She also burned the newspapers every day to prevent her grandson reading about a scandalous divorce case; but again he foiled her, fetching the papers from the Park gates and reading them before they reached the Lodge. It was a rather strange relationship. Once when he was six he said he wished his parents had lived. His grandmother answered that it was very fortunate for him that they had died. Her words, as he put it, 'made a disagreeable impression on me'.

While Frank was at school and when Bertie was six, their grandfather died. Frank was brought home, and his brother was surprised and delighted to see him drive up in a cab, in the middle of term. 'Hurrah!' he called out. But he was quickly called to order. 'Hush!' said his nurse, 'you mustn't say "Hurrah" today.' That was the least of it. Frank and

Bertrand Russell, tragically orphaned before he was four, was brought up by his grandparents at Pembroke Lodge in Richmond Park. A visitor described it as 'an unsuitable place for children', and remembered Bertie as 'a solemn little boy in a blue velvet suit'.

his uncle were the chief mourners, and had to spend two long days sitting in a brougham behind the hearse on its slow journey to Chenies in Buckinghamshire, where for over three centuries the Russells had been buried. His grandfather's death brought another change for Frank. 'I was no longer Viscount Amberley,' he groaned. 'I was Earl Russell – wretched child of twelve!'

Nevertheless, there were some good moments to come for both boys. These included a family holiday in Perthshire about a year later. Frank's uncle taught him about electricity, sparking off a passionate interest. They experimented with telegraphy, and the girl at the local post office let him send and take messages on a real post office instrument. He was in ecstasies. 'I don't think I had experienced anything like it', he wrote later, 'since at the age of eight I was left in sole charge of a threshing machine.'

Bertie was not much older when he discovered a passion as engrossing as Frank's love of machinery. When he was eleven, his brother began to teach him Euclid. The experience was, he said, 'one of the great events of my life, as dazzling as first love. I had not imagined that there was anything so delicious in the world.' It also helped him to believe that he might have some intelligence. From that moment mathematics was his 'chief interest and source of happiness'. Algebra he found a much harder nut to crack, and on one occasion drove his tutor to the point of throwing the book at his pupil's head. Once again, Lady Russell frustrated her grandson with her kind but mistaken intentions. She was afraid that he would over-work, and insisted that lessons should be short. So he had to sit at the desk in his room and carry on by candlelight, on the *qui-vive* so that if anyone turned up he could blow out the candle and jump into bed. Among the few encouragements that came his way were some words he had with Dr Jowett, the Master of Balliol, who was the first person to show the boy that he thought he was intelligent, and so made him resolve to achieve 'something of intellectual importance'.

Of all the topics that were taboo at Pembroke Lodge, sex headed the list; the others, according to Frank, were birth, swearing, trade, money and passion. Religion might be mentioned, but only in suitably hushed tones. Bertie described the loneliness and misery of his adolescence in his grandmother's house, and how her taboos forced him to be deceitful. When he was twelve a friend told him about sex, and a little later his tutor said that he would soon experience an important physical change.

He urgently needed to know more, but who would tell him? He and a friend had recourse to a page-boy who was better informed than they were, but this was discovered, judged to be a grave offence, and Bertie was sent to bed on a bread-and-water diet. 'Strange to say,' he commented later, 'this treatment did not destroy my interest in sex.'

He went on with his search for information, finding medical dictionaries as helpful as anything. (Evidently Frank was away at the time; otherwise he would surely have answered his brother's questions.) At fifteen Bertie began to experience intense sexual arousal and would be disturbed, as he sat working, by frequent erections. He allowed himself to masturbate, but resisted this as he felt it must be wrong. What he longed for was a sight of a naked female body, and he made several attempts at spying on the maids as they were undressing, but always without success. Inspired by their thwarted desires, he made with a friend what he called an 'underground house', kissed and hugged a housemaid in it, and asked her if she would like to spend a night with him. Her answer shook him: she would rather die, she said. His reaction was not, as might be thought, that he had been rejected; he was just convinced of his own sinfulness.

Religion was no less confusing than sex. Bertie's grandfather was Anglican, his grandmother a Scottish Presbyterian who after a time became a Unitarian. He was taken one Sunday to the Episcopalian local parish church, the next to the Presbyterian service, and at home his teaching was Unitarian. No wonder he gradually lost his faith in religion, in life after death, and finally in God. He was reading voraciously, but he had to be secretive about this too and about any notes he wanted to make on his thinking. He achieved this by writing English words in Greek letters. This inadequate home education till he was sixteen was inflicted on Bertie mainly because his grandfather had wanted the boys to escape the 'contamination' of a public school. Frank thought that this made his brother, until he went to Cambridge, 'an unendurable little prig'. It was an additional handicap that the tutors who came to teach him seldom stayed longer than three months. Why was this? Bertie himself thought it was because he had to enlist their help in hiding things from his family, and this put them in a very awkward position. His summing-up could hardly be more damning: 'After the age of fourteen I found living at home only endurable at the cost of complete silence about everything that interested me.' What could be further from his parents' enlightened ideals?

But the Russells were not the boys' only grandparents. They also visited their maternal grandmother, Lady Stanley at Alderley, and had curiously opposite reactions to her and her family. Frank was the only grandchild who was not afraid of the old matriarch – even though when he was very young she made him read aloud to her in French, and rapped his knuckles with a heavy paper-knife at every mispronunciation. But he found it a relief to escape from the repressed hush of the Russell household to the noisy, argumentative meals and gatherings at the Stanley home in Dover Street. They also understood his interests, taking him to the Lectures for Juveniles at the Royal Institution nearby, to Westminster Abbey, St Paul's, the Tower of London, the Bank of England, the Mint, the Zoo, Madame Tussaud's, pantomimes and theatres. Lady Stanley and her unmarried daughter enlisted Frank in their good works, and he enjoyed helping to teach the rowdy classes in his aunt's 'ragged night school' in Soho.

For some reason Bertie's visits to Lady Stanley were less successful. He was shy, she was notoriously fierce, so he became just one of the many frightened grandchildren. On a famous occasion in a crowded drawing-room when he was about twelve, she listed some well-known books. Had he read them? No, not a single one, and Lady Stanley turned in despair to her visitors. 'I have no intelligent grandchildren', she complained. He said later that he thought, in retrospect, that her words 'acted as a stimulus' to him, though at the time he felt completely crushed. Only once did Bertie feel he had pleased her. She could express her approval as majestically as her contempt, and when he asked for *Tristram Shandy* as a birthday present, she presented her grandson with an autographed first edition.

18

The Lytteltons and Gladstones at Hagley and Hawarden

Whatever made such a genius as Tolstoy start one of the greatest of novels by saying that all happy families are alike? The two nineteenth-century families who are the subject of this chapter were happy in a very unusual way; and though they just happen to be in many ways rather like Tolstoy's greatest family – the Rostovs of *War and Peace* – there are certainly plenty of happy families who are very different from them.

To begin with, the Lytteltons and the Gladstones were exceptionally 'well connected'. Then their mothers were two sisters who from birth to death were deeply devoted to each other – they and their husbands shared a double wedding in 1839 – so that their children grew up together, more like one family than two. Catherine and Mary Glynne could claim among their ancestors Charlemagne, William the Conqueror and Edward I, as well as at least six eminent English statesmen. Mary's husband was George, fourth Baron Lyttelton; Catherine married a commoner, William Ewart Gladstone, but he was already doing well in the House of Commons and was to become one of the great politicians of his day, four times Prime Minister and honoured almost universally in his old age as the 'G.O.M.', the country's Grand Old Man. (Queen Victoria, always charmed by Gladstone's adversary, Disraeli, was among the few who refused to acknowledge his qualities both during his lifetime and after his death.)

Like most Victorian brides, Catherine and Mary soon became mothers of a large family. Seven Lyttelton babies were born during the 1840s, and the Gladstones kept pace, producing six during the first ten years of their marriage. It is mainly because Lucy, the second Lyttelton daughter, kept a diary from the age of thirteen until her husband, Lord Frederick Cavendish, was murdered in Ireland twenty-eight years later,

189

that the two families can now be seen so clearly in all their goings-on – in their joys and griefs, at their lessons and parties and prayers. The Gladstones were thought to be more earnest, the Lytteltons sprightlier, though they too were unfailingly earnest about two things – the Church and cricket. The Lytteltons' family home was a pedimented, towered square mansion called Hagley Hall, between Birmingham and the Welsh hills; the Gladstones were based on Hawarden Castle, the recently modernized mediaeval stronghold which came to them through their mother's family, and was not far away, near Chester. Both families also had homes in London. They met continually, parents, children, nurses and governesses migrating across country, almost like members of a long-established travelling circus, and settling into the familiar quarters in the other house with just that spice of variety that made each visit something of a treat.

For the youngest children, the nursery must have seemed their whole world. A close-up view of the Lytteltons' London nursery in the 1840s comes in Lucy's diary, and much of what it shows must apply to the two country nurseries also. She remembered its

two windows; the work-table, much battered, dirty red, with a curious round hole in it that I was always poking my finger through, standing in one; a high white cupboard where the toys were kept, in the other, with flower-pots standing on the top. A massive, towering, white wardrobe, with deep drawer forming its lower part, stood in one corner, filled with frocks, linen, etc; and where the ornamental pin-cushion, little basket, christening cap, powder-box, etc., was always kept before an expected Baby required them. A dark wood cupboard, also a great height and based by drawers, against one wall, wherein the breakfast, dinner, and tea things were kept, with cold plum-pudding wont to be preserved from the servants' supper. The fireplace on your left as you go in, with a heavy carved old-fashioned mantel-shelf; half-way up the wall two large rows of bookshelves hung up, whereon grotesque china ornaments, superior toys only played with on grand occasions, and a very few books stood, the latter consisted of a portentous family medicine-book and suchlike drab-coloured volumes. A large map, always my great delight, representing all the birds, beasts, and fish imaginable, and many old prints of foreign men and women, the principal picture being one of the Queen and the Duchess of Kent, standing as if they were about to set off on a polka, completed the decoration of the walls. In early times a swing hung from the ceiling; the hooks used for that purpose remain there now. By the fireplace stood a little low rocking-chair wherein I fancy we have all been sent to sleep. The middle table was round, the carpet and paper bright.

So much for the London scene. At Hagley the younger children crowded into a big nursery at the top of the house, graduating at about seven to the more studious surroundings of the schoolroom. This was unusual in not being also stowed away upstairs; instead it formed a kind of passageway between George Lyttelton's study and his wife's boudoir, so that parents and children were continually in touch with each other as part of the mechanics of everyday life. Nothing could have been more different from those families whose nannies brought the children down, dressed up and tidied, to see their parents in the drawing-room after tea. Mary Lyttelton would smile as she passed through the schoolroom. 'You little pigs!' or 'Absurd monkeys!' their father would say.

So the double family was a sprawling, affectionate group of – eventually – nineteen boys and girls, broken up in term-time when the boys were old enough for school and left the girls to a succession of governesses and visiting tutors. George Lyttelton wrote a good description of them all, describing the experience of

> entering a room at Hagley or Hawarden during one of those great confluences of families which occur among the Glynnes, and finding seventeen children upon the floor under the age of twelve, and consequently all inkstands, books, carpets, furniture, ornaments, in intimate intermixture and in every form of fraction and confusion.

Both families were linked by the 'Glynnese' ancestry they shared. They also used the word to describe their private family language, a humorous and allusive mixture of real and invented words which Catherine and Mary handed on to their husbands and children. In 1851 George Lyttelton published *The Glynnese Glossary*, giving definitions of all the meanings, with some irreverent sidelights on Gladstone and his occasional lapses into the family lingo. Some of the words and expressions – bathing-feel, grubous, mawkin, phanted and passing pigman, to take a random sample – are gibberish to the uninitiated. Others, like being 'over the moon', are now a part of our language.

Lucy looked back on her childhood as on 'a bright, unruffled river'. At twelve she saw herself as 'a heedless tomboy of a child, the worry of the servants, and the ruthless destroyer of frocks', redeemed only by a 'mixture of religious feeling and poetical fancies'. She might have mentioned in her favour that she was also informed and sympathetic about important events of the day and sensitive to other people's lives. Her diary tells of the horror of the cholera epidemic, the resignation of Lord John Russell, and the Charge of the Light Brigade. She scolded herself when she left out an important piece of news. 'Oh, what a wretch I am!' she wrote penitently in September, 1855. 'If I haven't forgotten to put in the grand news!! SEBASTOPOL HAS FALLEN!'

The diary records other failings of Lucy's too. When she suspected herself of vanity – a weakness disapproved of strongly by both families – she designed her own punishment to fit the crime, and cut off her eyelashes because she thought they were the cause of her sin. Her judgment of herself as 'very unhappy, very ill-managed, and very naughty' does not altogether tally with the affectionate entries describing, for instance, the end of the school term, with the joy of 'seeing the dear boys' faces again' and having them at home, 'so jolly for their holidays, talking of carn't, harf, and clarse like anything'. (Lucy makes an interesting phonetic point here, as the boys were bringing home a new and strange sound, while she herself is believed to have pronounced a short 'a' – saying 'can't' to rhyme with 'rant', for instance – to the end of her life.)

The holidays were great times for them all. On the first day of 1857, Lucy's diary tells how 'the whole tribe of Gladstones poured into the house today and we make up the goodly number of 18 children under 17'. The next day there is a further picture of Hagley:

> The dear old house is choked, overflowing, echoing with children. The meals are the fun. Breakfasts are composed on 2 tables, a loaf and a half or 2 loaves, a plate of bread and butter, 3 or 4 good-sized pats of butter, two teapots, a dish of meat, a dish of bacon, and a toast-rack full. They are attended by Miss Smith, presiding at the top of one of the tables, dispensing drinkables, me at the bottom, dispensing meat, bacon, and butter, and cutting hunches of bread like a machine; at the top of the other table, Meriel presiding.

She goes on to describe the noise they all made: conversation, added to the clatter of crockery, the pouring of tea, hewing of bread and 'scrumping of jaws'.

At other times life at Hagley was quieter and simpler. Often the

The Lytteltons outside Hagley in 1863. From left to right: Alfred, Lucy, Neville, Arthur, Charles, Meriel, May, Spencer, Edward, Lavinia, Albert, and Robert.

Hagley was always full of children. In 1857 Lucy Lyttelton wrote in her diary that they had 'the goodly number of 18 children under 17' there – Lytteltons and their Gladstone cousins. Twenty-eight years afterwards a later generation was seen in front of the conservatory windows: only fifteen of them, 'as we did not have the 7 children under 2 years old photographed'.

children had only bread and butter for breakfast and tea, and nothing at all to eat between tea and breakfast the next morning. A parent or visitor who made his way to the square, high nursery on the third floor could be sure of finding 'always a baby to be washed and dressed before the fire'. As the Lytteltons were less well off than their Gladstone cousins, relations who visited Hagley often contributed to the housekeeping funds and the children wore handed-down and mended clothes. Both families travelled third-class on the railways in days when such carriages were often crowded, uncomfortable and smelly. The Lytteltons were aware that their father was worried at having so many mouths to feed and future careers to launch. 'Oh, such a break!' Lucy rejoiced in 1856. Her nine-year-old brother had been given an estate in New Zealand, so he was now a landed proprietor, 'and a whole son taken off Papa's hands'.

All four of the Lyttelton and Gladstone parents were exceptionally close to their children, spending more time with them and sharing their activities much more than was usual in those days. George Lyttelton was deeply distressed at partings from his children. When his eldest son first went to Eton, his father went with him and it was he who was the more upset, weeping uncontrollably at their room at an inn; and he was just as wretched when another son went off, when he was twelve, to join H.M.S. *Actaeon* at Portsmouth and not see his family again for three long years.

The Gladstones were just as devoted parents. Later, when Catherine wrote the introduction to *Early Influences*, a Victorian handbook on bringing up children, she insisted on the importance of parents knowing their children really well. She was preaching what she had already practised. She gave her children their first Bible lessons, and also taught them when they were away, without a governess, on holiday in Scotland. She too found it agonizing to send her boys off to boarding-school. She was specially fond of her two youngest sons – she called them her 'sugar-plums' – and dreaded the end of the holidays. 'I call it a kind of slow poison,' she wrote, 'one going after another, and the little boys' departure hanging over our head.' But she steeled herself to bear it. The sugar-plums, aged nine and ten, tried on their smart new jackets and trousers. 'On Sunday they beg to go to church in their school clothes,' Catherine wrote, 'and I mean to be very brave.'

And brave she could be. She proved this when she and Gladstone together nursed their young daughters through dangerous illnesses and when one of them, after agonizing meningitis, eventually died. She also had the courage – necessary because her husband was so often away – to punish the children when she thought this necessary. They later described how this was done by 'Mamma armed with a Japanese fan'. That does not sound very daunting, but it will be seen that Catherine could also inflict more formidable penalties. Both parents disliked doing this, and agreed that affection and example were more effective than the Japanese fan. Catherine put this theory to the test years later, when a seven-year-old great-nephew had been naughty. It seemed wrong and stupid to lock him in his room, so instead Catherine gave him a drum. All his life the boy remembered the lesson, as well as the image of a great-aunt who was 'adored and adorable'.

She was not always so understanding. Nor was she the only Victorian mother to take it upon herself to decide what was best for her daughters. She realized that Mary was both bright and musical, but did not get her the teachers she needed. (In her own youth Catherine had had piano lessons from no less a person than Franz Liszt.) Helen, too, was intelligent, but Catherine decided that she must concentrate on mastering government ciphers so that she could help her father by transcribing official telegrams. She also stood between another daughter and her chosen career: Agnes had often been on hospital visits with her mother, and wanted to be a nurse. But no. The sordid realities of hospital life would, Catherine decided, be too distressing; so Agnes accepted the classic role of compliant nineteenth-century daughter, and stayed at home until – at nearly the eleventh hour – she eventually married. All Catherine's sons were free, of course, to make their own decisions about their careers.

Both Gladstones agreed that their children must not be allowed to become self-indulgent or feel privileged by their father's eminence or their mother's ancestry. They too needed to economize at one time, and they wanted their family to have some experience of material realities. Catherine looked beautiful and distinguished, whatever she wore, and this may be partly why she expected her children to wear clothes that were sometimes shabby or unbecoming. Her endless involvement in 'good works' gave them some valuable lessons in practical philanthropy. During the Crimean War, the girls of both families made mufflers and shirts, and sent off parcels to the troops; and during the 'cotton famine' in Lancashire, the children were all enlisted to write begging letters on behalf of the soup-kitchen Catherine had started and the girls she brought to Hawarden to be trained for domestic work. Later, she opened her own homes to any needy children, even if they came straight from the cholera wards. So the children came to be aware of the hardship in the outside world. But while they were still young, the intricacies of politics were harder to master. 'Do tell me,' a friend once asked them, 'is your father a Whig or a Tory?' That was too difficult. 'I don't know,' Mary answered, 'but Dizzy's a Beast...'

Politics inevitably kept Gladstone often in London, so it was on Catherine's broad shoulders that the main weight of family responsibility fell. When he was at home, Catherine insisted that the first rule for the whole household was that 'Papa's work must not be interrupted'. His study at Hawarden was known in the family as 'the Temple of Peace', but his own and the Lyttelton children were allowed to crowd in – as long as not a word was spoken. One of his nieces told how sometimes – was it when the great man was not too hard pressed? or when the silence became unbearable? – he himself 'would *begin* a little talk to our great pride and some nervousness'. What did they talk about? Problems they had met in their Bible reading, Roman Catholicism, and appreciation of beautiful scenery, poetry and music – not the easiest or most appetizing of menus. But Gladstone could also be light-hearted and demonstrative. He often played with the children, hugged and cuddled them, gave them rides on his back, and joined them when they were making a giant snowman. It has been suggested that he had a reason as well as a wish to do this, as he himself never remembered being kissed by his own father and perhaps blamed this for the sense of sexual and other guilt that haunted him throughout his life.

Gladstone's niece, Lavinia, described a specially good game her uncle played when all the children were together at Hawarden. One of the boys remarked that the Bishop of Chester was the ugliest man he knew. Oh no, said another; the Dean is much uglier. 'Upon which Uncle William divided us into 2 parties as in the H. of C. with Speaker & all, & made an absurd speech himself dwelling on the marked features & the plain looks in the 2 men with eloquent choice of adjectives.' This was followed by a debate, counting of votes and announcing of the final decision.

There are other attractive shots of Gladstone as a father. With his eldest son he went walking and climbing in Wales, covering as many as forty miles at a stretch, and on one occasion enjoying some good talk with a pedlar they met on their way. He seems to have been more sensitive than their mother was to the children's talents and aspirations. While Mary was still hardly more than a baby, he understood how musical she was; and he had an intimate talk with his son Stephen before he was twelve, when the boy told his father his dream of one day being a clergyman 'if he could see how to manage the sermons'.

Gladstone's relationship to his children had much in common with that of the other Tory Prime Minister at Hatfield, a house they all knew well. Just as the young Cecils called their father 'a goose', so the Hawarden children were altogether undaunted by the eminent statesman in their midst. 'We treated him with scant respect,' his daughter Mary remembered, 'argued across him while he was talking; even contradicted him.' There was a family habit of shouting out 'A lie! A lie!' when they disagreed with something that was said, and there was general amusement at the expression on the face of John Morley, Gladstone's admirer and biographer, the first time he heard one of the great man's opinions greeted so roughly. But of course both families loved him all the more for being so easy with them. 'Who wouldn't enjoy a walk with Uncle William?' Lucy asked. 'Able to answer any question you ask him.' And an entry in Mary's diary reads: 'Papa at home, very snug'; and there is another, a little later – children's tastes have certainly changed – 'snug evening analysing the Pharisees'.

The younger ones saw less of their father, of course, as by then he was often away in London, and when he was at home it seems that the Temple of Peace was not quite so open to the family. There is a description of the two youngest boys, when it was time to visit their father in his room, waiting at the door 'like little dogs who never resent exclusion but are overjoyed when they are allowed in'. They were proud that their Papa was a famous statesman, but to them he was also someone who sang funny songs, recited 'Fee fi fo fum' terrifyingly and melodramatically, and crossed one leg over the other to give them rides on his foot to the accompaniment of 'Ride a cock horse to Banbury Cross'. He played Commerce with them, wielded a hefty bat, and treated them to teaspoons of black coffee. He could always get on his young sons' wave-length – or was it more a question of switching them on to his own? – and they enjoyed discussions with him, learning to think things out for themselves and feeling free to contradict him. There were no holds barred – except untruthfulness.

But the family picture cannot be complete without a reminder of how nineteenth-century parents – even the most loving – punished their

Gladstone with his wife and children at Hawarden.

children. And what they punished them for. Lucy Lyttelton's naughtinesses included stealing an apple and some cold plum-pudding, and cutting off a lock of her hair and then saying that one of the boys had done it. When her mother thought the children had been unkind, vain or quarrelsome – three of the family's cardinal sins – she would take them into their father's room and put their 'small tender hands under a thing for pressing letters together...This was done very solemnly, Mamma shaking her head slowly at us all the time...oh, the disgrace!' Lucy was also 'continually' put between the heavy double doors of the house and left there; she was 'often whipped', and her 'usual punishment was being put for a time into a large, deep, old-fashioned bath that was in one corner of the schoolroom', partly in the dark.

But these were small trials compared with the tragedy that awaited them. The doctor warned that Mary, after having had eleven children, would be unlikely to survive another pregnancy. After that there was a slight pause, but eventually a twelfth child arrived, and six months later Mary died. No one seems to have thought that this might perhaps have been avoided, that anything other than the divine will could have been the reason why a woman in her early forties should die after having all those children in less than twenty years. 'It is of no use – God has set His seal', wrote Lucy in her diary. Late at night the children were taken, some of them only half awake, to say goodbye to their mother. 'Bless you dears,' she said to them, 'Mammy is going away.' To her six-year-old son she said: 'Arthur dear, I am going to heaven I hope.' He wept bitterly, and said later that he would like to go there with her, if she could not stay at Hagley with him.

In those days they were not in the habit of resolving that death should have no dominion. All the blinds in the house were drawn, a huge hatchment was raised over the door in the hall, and everyone stayed indoors. The maids set to work at once to make mourning clothes, and in these the children all went to the funeral, walking lugubriously to church, hand in hand, in pairs. They must have looked like the figures on a medieval memorial brass. Sad though they all were, it was too much to bear. Lucy told how delighted they were to have 'the house light again and hearing the boys whistle'. But of course life could never be the same. The eldest daughter took her mother's place, and she and Lucy did all they could for the younger children. As each girl married and left home, the next one took over. The last in the relay race was only fifteen. No wonder the girls felt daunted at 'having to scold or "have a little talk" with the maidservants now and then'. Once when Lucy had been reading to her little brothers from some improving book about self-denial, she asked one of them to take some broth to the village. 'O, but I wanted to go and slide!' the little boy protested, probably having already had more than his fill of morality. Lucy reminded him of what they had been reading. 'O, I forgot!' he said, with a blush; and he delivered the broth with a good grace.

So religion – even more than cricket – was the foundation of their upbringing. 'Church is Lucy's public house,' they used to say. 'It is impossible to keep her out of it.' One Sunday in church at Hawarden, when she was thirteen, she had some kind of mystical experience which she felt would always remain with her. It flashed on her 'like a blinding light, a great thought of Eternity as bearing upon myself'. A year or two later, kept in bed with a sore throat, she complained: 'I do so pity myself, feeling quite well, and a whole Sunday without any church! Last Sunday in Lent too. Oh!' Soon after that she was confirmed by the Archbishop of Canterbury, and she felt that for her 'the new Life' had begun. For the others, too, religion was a constant presence. When one of the children was seriously ill, they all joined in prayer just as they did – grown-ups and children together – when Mary safely gave birth to her last baby.

The young children, of course, saw even more of their nurse than their parents. A much-loved nanny called Newman – but generally known as 'Newmanny' – came to the Lytteltons in 1840 for their first child and stayed, commanding a succession of nurserymaids, for the rest of her life. It was she who presided over the great gatherings when both families came together. She sang nursery songs and hymns to them, dosed them when medicines were needed (and sometimes when they were not), went on holiday with the children at seaside lodgings and, after Mary's death, mothered the three youngest boys. It was Newmanny, when she had been with the family thirty-five years, who nursed the youngest Lyttelton daughter when she was dying of typhoid fever; Newmanny's name was the one she called upon most often, and the last word she spoke.

An interesting sidelight on Newman's position in the family is that no one seems to have asked her opinion about a great opportunity that might have been hers. Lord Lyttelton's mother, after her husband died, became Lady of the Bedchamber to Queen Victoria, and later was governess to the royal children. In 1842 she told her daughter-in-law that the Queen would like to have Newman in the Palace nursery. Mary wrote about this to her husband: 'Of course, I would not be so selfish as to think of keeping Newman, if by giving her up it would add the least to Ly L's comfort or be of advantage to the poor little children at the Palace.' Lady Lyttelton must have been told how invaluable Newman was to her son's family, for the matter was dropped. But did Newman ever hear anything of a proposal which might, after all, have been much more important to her than to Lady Lyttelton or those 'poor little children at the Palace'?

Newman's kingdom was the nursery. The schoolroom and lessons – for the girls, and for the boys until they went away to school – were ruled over by various governesses. They found the children unevenly grounded: one little Gladstone girl was reading 'easy stories' when she was four and yet, when a late Lyttelton baby was born, the younger children had been told nothing about it and so were 'at first incredulous and then over the moon'. The governesses too were a varied lot. Loving mother though Catherine Gladstone was, she allowed hers a very free rein, and seems not to have thought of doing a little market research to discover how her daughters were being treated. It also seems strange that, agonized though she was at sending her sons off to school so young, she either did not know about, or did not prevent, their being very unhappy, often beaten, and kept on very short rations at their prep school. Catherine's daughter Mary said that her governesses destroyed her self-confidence by never giving her a word of praise and by belittling her music. 'My governess, from 10 to 17 years, continued to treat me as half-witted, so I grew up as a nonentity. I have never outgrown it,' she remembered in her seventies. Throughout her schoolroom days, she met with constant disapproval. Like Bertrand Russell when, late in his teens, he gathered from a talk with Dr Jowett that he showed signs of intelligence, Mary never questioned her governess's low opinion of her until one day she came into a room unexpectedly and heard her piano playing described as 'quite glorious'.

The Lyttelton schoolroom was equally discouraging. Lucy's governesses sound positively sadistic. There was one who whipped her for obstinacy when she was 'only dense', punished her too often, and let her see how much she preferred her sisters. When they were on holiday together in Brighton, she took Lucy for a walk with her hands tied behind her back and frightened her by saying they were sure to meet a policeman. The girls were delighted when this terror was replaced by a 'pretty, gentle, little lady' who proved easy, loving and loved in return. The only punishment she ever gave them was learning poetry by heart, and this they seldom did. Lucy admitted that they ' "shirked" duties, and became untruthful, dishonest, and self-conceited'. More discipline was needed, so a stricter governess was found and shirking stopped.

Perhaps it was not altogether a pleasure to be governess to the Lyttelton girls. When Lucy was fourteen, her diary tells of the arrival of 'the new French woman, more hugely fat than imagination can picture, or tongue describe'. Lessons now became very regular, 'but nevertheless the squabble, the chatter, the clatter, the laughing, the scolding, the crossness, the "Do this, Don't do that, Go there, Come here" that goes on all the time is quite bewildering'. Through it all the girls seem to have kept a certain independence of judgement. They read Shakespeare – duly expurgated by Thomas Bowdler, of course – and put him in the dock. They liked some of the plays, but Lucy did not 'care for' *All's Well that Ends Well* or *A Midsummer Night's Dream*, and she pronounced that '*Love's Labour's Lost* is trash.'

The fat French governess did not last a year, and after her came 'a nice real comfortable English one, ladylike and pleasant-looking'. She set them a full programme. On Mondays and Thursdays they did Italian, reading Metastasio and the plays of Goldoni, learning verbs, translating, and talking together in Italian. On Tuesdays and Fridays they had French, and read Lamartine, learned and recited passages from Racine, wrote to dictation, and translated Bossuet's *Histoire Universelle* into English and then back again into French. They did an hour's music every day, learned English poetry and recited it by heart, and read and made a précis of a book about Rome. English composition and history, geography, arithmetic, 'dates' and word-definitions were also on the menu.

So much for lessons. After that it is a pleasant change to see how the children enjoyed themselves. They were good at this: it was all part of their affectionate, high-spirited way of life. On Lavinia's ninth birthday, they all crowned her with flowers and ivy and she was 'taken round the house with huzzas'. For both families, just to be at home was enough to make them happy. 'I am glad for you to be at dear old Hagley,' a Gladstone wrote to her Lyttelton cousin in 1863. 'I am hoping to go to Hawarden in a month, greater bliss to me than anyone can tell.' Lucy, even after her marriage had brought her many happy visits to Chatsworth, always remembered the 'glorious summers' of her childhood at Hagley, walking and riding in the country, driving with their mother in the pony-carriage, sitting under the trees or on the lawn, and 'in the evenings, coming to dessert in the high cool dining-room, and sitting on the perron out of doors till the first stars came out'. In the winter there were roaring fires in the wide grates, and they went sliding with the boys or else played round the fire in the library.

They played dozens of different games. The Lyttelton boys inherited their father's passion for cricket, so the pitch had pride of place in the garden, right outside the drawing-room windows. Their sisters, dragooned into fielding and picking up balls, were less enthusiastic. Rain never stopped play for the boys: the younger ones went on in an upstairs corridor, stuffing a leather ball with bran and using a paper-knife as a bat. The older ones, with characteristic Lyttelton unawareness of the treasures of Hagley, batted and fielded among the delicate plasterwork, paintings and glass of the Long Gallery, until Catherine Gladstone eventually protested about this.

Among the most violent games were family napkin fights. All of a sudden George Lyttelton would, during a meal, give a loud bellow and hurl his napkin, rolled into a ball, in the face of one of his sons. All the boys then joined in the bellowing and hurling, and soon there was such a shindy that one guest is said to have sought sanctuary on the (no doubt priceless) sideboard. Calmer games were battledore and shuttlecock and croquet, which seems to have been a novelty for them, as Lucy calls it 'a nice Irish game introduced here' by the new governess. When they were in London there were different delights, though there too they rode, and there is a nostalgic pleasure in hearing how one outing with the horses in Rotten Row brought them home by way of Piccadilly and Pall Mall.

In London the children were taken to the theatre to hear Fanny Kemble read Shakespeare and – probably because of their grand-mother's Palace connections – some of them were invited to the children's balls at Court. One sister had her hair curl-papered every night for a week for one of these. (That could be a painful process, and history does not record whether it was worth it.) Lucy has left a detailed account of the Queen's Ball for Children she went to, with her sister and one of the Gladstone girls, when she was fourteen. A hairdresser came to wash and 'do' their hair an hour or so before half-past eight, when they were due at Buckingham Palace. Lucy and her cousin wore dresses which she describes as 'something magnificent. A beautiful muslin frock trimmed with ruches and daisies. White silk stockings, white satin shoes with white bows, white kid gloves trimmed with white daisies and a wreath of two rows of daisies'. The Ball was in honour of the four-year-old Prince Arthur, and all the girls curtseyed as the Queen passed. 'Oh, ecstasy,' Lucy warbled to her diary, 'she shook hands with me! imagine my feelings and my curtsey; I kept hold of her dear hand as long as I dared.'

But one thing had been missing from Lucy's preparations. The Prince of Wales asked Lucy if she could dance the valse: alas, she could not, so he partnered Agnes Gladstone instead. The following year there were more Court festivities. In April Lucy went to the Queen's Ball in honour of Princess Alice's birthday; it began at nine, at supper they had wine, seltzer water and delicious ices, and half an hour after midnight all was over. Four days later, at the end of May 1856, when the Crimean War had at last come to an end, they went to see the 'illuminations in honour of the Peace'. London had other diversions to offer them, too. One day her older sister went to hear a debate in the House of Lords while Lucy heard one in the Commons. 'It was one of the most delightful things to go to that I have ever been at!' she let her enthusiasm run away with her grammar.

As well as going to London and the two family country homes, there were also visits to other relations and family friends. The Gladstone and Balfour children often met, and both spent holidays together at Whittinghame, the Balfours' home in Scotland, and with the Cecils at Hatfield, where they enjoyed frightening each other with ghost stories in front of the vast log fire. The Queen's affection for Catherine Gladstone brought repeated invitations to her to bring her family to play with the royal children at Buckingham Palace and Windsor, as well as a proposal that the oldest Gladstone boy should go to Germany with the Prince of Wales. The children also had seaside holidays, as Catherine was a great believer in the health-giving powers of sea air. It seems strange now that a large family could contemplate moving from their own large and healthy house, to squeeze into cramped and uncomfortable seaside rooms. Yet the Lytteltons with two friends and a full complement of nurses, maids and governesses did this during the winter of 1855–6, when Mary was ill-advisedly pregnant and badly in need of rest. One little bedroom was shared by the three girls, and an even smaller one by Newman and the baby. A modest living-room had to house another girl's bed as well as being used during the day by the children and for the washing. Even if three of the children had not caught scarlet fever there, it is difficult to see how the visit could possibly have brought their mother rest and health.

After that it must have been specially good to get back to Hagley. Home was where almost all the best things happened. At Christmas, for instance, the children sang 'Hark the Herald Angels' at each door, starting with their parents', whose bed they jumped into for hugs and kisses, and 'ending with the nurseries, where we all assembled to drink coffee and eat tea-cake, surrounded by the admiring maids, with the holly all round the room shining in the firelight'. At Hawarden, too. Christmas was a great occasion, with local schoolchildren, villagers and farmers all invited to enjoy the sparkling tree in the library, with high tea in the drawing-room and ale in the servants' hall. Even when Mary was within only a couple of months of giving birth to her last child, and less than a year before she died, the whole crowd of Gladstones came to Hagley for Christmas. Sixteen of the children – aged from three to late teens – took part in grand-scale theatricals. Both mothers were aware of the tragedy that was probably lying ahead. But they did not let it dim the Christmas lights, and it seemed that never had the two families been happier.

Farewell to the Nursery

And so the nursery door closes on a way of life that will certainly never be seen again, one that hardly anyone would ever want to see again. Yet at the time it seemed good and desirable enough to many people, and most of those who still remember it agree with them. Those who questioned it raised their eyebrows gently, as Robert Louis Stevenson did in *A Child's Garden of Verses*:

> It is very nice to think
> The world is full of meat and drink,
> With little children saying grace
> In every Christian kind of place.

And again:

> The child that is not clean and neat,
> With lots of toys and things to eat,
> He is a naughty child, I'm sure ...
> Or else his dear papa is poor.

It has been interesting and enlightening – and often amusing and touching as well – to visit those noble nurseries of the nineteenth century and to compare the children who woke and slept, played and learned, laughed and cried in them with those of today. Reading or writing about other people's lives means sharing those lives to some extent, and sharing other people's lives often (if not always) prompts warm feelings of sympathy and affection. The researching and writing of this book have also prompted a regret that time is a one-way street, so that I cannot return the hospitality of those Georgian and Victorian parents by inviting them to meet their great-grandchildren of the 1980s. What surprises and shocks they would have! And perhaps a little wistfulness and admiration too?

Bibliography

Alsop, Susan Mary, *Lady Sackville: a Biography*, Weidenfeld and Nicolson, 1976

Argyll, eighth Duke of (George Douglas Campbell), *Autobiography and Memoirs*, John Murray, 1906

Askwith, Betty, *The Lytteltons: a Family Chronicle of the Nineteenth Century*, Chatto and Windus, 1975
Piety and Wit: a Biography of Harriet Countess Granville, Collins, 1982

Balsan, Consuelo Vanderbilt (Consuelo Spencer Churchill), *The Glitter and the Gold*, Heinemann, 1953

Battiscombe, Georgina (Georgina Harwood), *Mrs Gladstone*, Constable, 1956
Shaftesbury, Constable, 1974

Berners, Lord (G.H. Tyrwhitt-Wilson), *First Childhood*, Constable, 1934

Birkenhead, Earl of (F.W.F. Smith), *Halifax*, Hamish Hamilton, 1965

Blakiston, Georgiana, *Lord William Russell and his Wife*, John Murray, 1972

Blunden, Margaret, *The Countess of Warwick: a Biography*, Cassell, 1967

Bowen, Elizabeth, *Bowen's Court*, Longmans, 1964

Calder-Marshall, Arthur, *The Two Duchesses*, Hutchinson, 1978

Carroll, Lewis, *The Annotated Alice*, ed. Martin Gardner, Penguin, 1965
Diaries, ed. R. Lancelyn Green, Cassell, 1953

Cavendish, Lady Frederick, *The Diary of*, ed. John Bailey, John Murray, 1927

Cecil, Lord David, *The Cecils of Hatfield House*, Constable, 1973
Melbourne, Constable, 1965

Cecil, Lady Gwendolen, *Life of Robert Cecil, Marquess of Salisbury*, 4 vols, Hodder and Stoughton, 1921-32

Churchill, Winston, *My Early Life*, Thornton Butterworth, 1930
Lord Randolph Churchill, Odhams Press, 1952

Cooper, Lady Diana, *The Rainbow Comes and Goes*, Hart-Davis, 1958

Coxhead, Elizabeth, *Lady Gregory: a Literary Portrait*, Secker and Warburg, 1966

Craig, Mary, *Longford: a Biographical Portrait*, Hodder and Stoughton, 1978

Darroch, Sandra Jobson, *Ottoline: the Life of Lady Ottoline Morrell*, Chatto and Windus, 1976

Davidson, Angus, *Edward Lear*, John Murray, 1938

Drew, Mary, *Catherine Gladstone*, Nisbet and Co., 1919

Dugdale, Blanche, *Family Homespun*, John Murray, 1940

Eden, Emily, *Letters of*, ed. Violet Dickinson, Macmillan, 1919

Egremont, Lord (John Edward Reginald Wyndham), *Wyndham and Children First*, Macmillan, 1968

Egremont Max, *Balfour: a Life of Arthur James Balfour*, Collins, 1980
The Cousins: the Friendships, Opinions and Activities of Wilfrid Scawen Blunt and George Wyndham, Collins, 1977

Elwin, Malcolm, *Lord Byron's Wife*, Macdonald, 1962

Field, Mrs E.M., *The Child and his Book*, Wells Gardner, 1891

Fleming, Kate, *The Churchills*, Weidenfeld and Nicolson, 1975

Gattégno, Jean, *Lewis Carroll*, George Allen and Unwin, 1977

Glendinning, Victoria, *Edith Sitwell: a Unicorn Among Lions*, Weidenfeld and Nicolson, 1981

 Elizabeth Bowen: Portrait of a Writer, Weidenfeld and Nicolson, 1977

Guedalla, Philip, *The Duke*, Hodder and Stoughton, 1931

Gunn, Peter, *My Dearest Augusta*, Bodley Head, 1968

Hare, Augustus, *The Gurneys of Earlham*, George Allen, 1895

 The Story of my Life, 6 vols, George Allen, 1896-1900

Henley Dorothy, *Rosalind Howard, Countess of Carlisle*, Hogarth Press, 1958

Howard de Walden, Margherita, *Pages from my Life*, Sidgwick and Jackson, 1965

Howell-Thomas, Dorothy, *Lord Melbourne's Susan*, Gresham Books, 1978

Huxley, Gervas, *Lady Elizabeth and the Grosvenors*, Oxford University Press, 1965

 Victorian Duke, Oxford University Press, 1967

James, Robert Rhodes, *Rosebery*, Weidenfeld and Nicolson, 1963

Jersey, Countess of (Margaret Elizabeth Villiers), *Fifty-One Years of Victorian Life*, John Murray, 1922

Leconfield, Maud Lady (ed.), *Three Howard Sisters*, John Murray, 1955

Lehmann, John, *Edward Lear and his World*, Thames and Hudson, 1977

Lever, Sir Tresham, *The Herberts of Wilton*, John Murray, 1967

Longford Elizabeth, *Byron*, Weidenfeld and Nicolson, 1976

 Wellington: Pillar of State, Weidenfeld and Nicolson, 1972

Lytton, Robert, first Earl of, *Life, Letters and Literary Remains of Edward Bulwer, Lord Lytton*, Kegan Paul and Co., 1883

 Personal and Literary Letters, ed. Lady Betty Balfour, Longmans, 1906

MacCarthy, D. and Russell, Agatha, *Lady John Russell: a Memoir*, Methuen, 1910

Marchand, Leslie (ed.), *In My Hot Youth. Byron's Letters and Journals*, John Murray, 1973

Marlow, Joyce, *Mr and Mrs Gladstone: an Intimate Biography*, Weidenfeld and Nicolson, 1977

Martin, Ralph G., *Lady Randolph Churchill*, Cassell, 1969

Masterman, Lucy (Lucy Lyttelton) (ed.), *Mary Gladstone – Mrs Drew: Diaries and Letters*, Methuen, 1930

Masters, Brian, *The Dukes*, Blond and Briggs, 1975

Mathew, David, *Lord Acton and his Times*, Eyre and Spottiswoode, 1968

Milner, Viscountess V.G., *My Picture Gallery*, John Murray, 1951

Mitford, Nancy (ed.), *The Ladies of Alderley*, Hamish Hamilton, 1938

 The Stanleys of Alderley. Letters, 1851-65, Hamish Hamilton, 1939

Moore, Doris Langley, *Ada, Countess of Lovelace, Byron's Legitimate Daughter*, John Murray, 1977

 The Late Lord Byron, John Murray, 1961

Newman, Aubrey, *The Stanhopes of Chevening*, Macmillan, 1969

Nicolson, Nigel, *Mary Curzon*, Weidenfeld and Nicolson, 1977

 Portrait of a Marriage, Weidenfeld and Nicolson, 1973

Oman, Carola, *The Gascoyne Heiress*, Hodder and Stoughton, 1968

Pollock, Alice, *Portrait of my Victorian Youth*, Johnson Publications, 1971

Powell, Violet, *Margaret, Countess of Jersey: a Biography*, Heinemann, 1978

Roberts, Brian, *The Mad Bad Line: the Family of Lord Alfred Douglas*, Hamish Hamilton, 1981

Roberts, Charles, *The Radical Countess: the History of the Life of Rosalind, Countess of Carlisle*, Steel Bros, 1962

Rose, Kenneth, *The Later Cecils*, Weidenfeld and Nicolson, 1975

Russell, Bertrand, *Autobiography*, George Allen and Unwin, 1967

Russell, Bertrand and Patricia (eds), *The Amberley Papers*, Hogarth Press, 1937

Russell, George W.E., *Collections and Recollections*, Nelson, 1908

One Look Back, Wells Gardner and Co., 1912

Russell, John Francis Stanley, Earl of, *My Life and Adventures*, Cassell, 1923

Sackville-West, V., *Pepita*, Hogarth Press, 1937

Sherwood, Mrs, *The Fairchild Family*, Wells Gardner and Co., 1931

Sitwell, Edith, *Taken Care of: an Autobiography*, Hutchinson, 1965

Sitwell, Osbert, *Left Hand, Right Hand!*, Macmillan, 1945

The Scarlet Tree, Macmillan, 1946

Wellington, first Duke of (Arthur Wellesley), *A Great Man's Friendship: Letters to Mary, Marchioness of Salisbury*, ed. Lady Burghclere (W.A.H.C. Gardner), John Murray, 1927

Wellington, seventh Duke of (Gerald Wellesley) (ed.), *Wellington and his Friends*, Macmillan, 1965

Westminster, Loelia, Duchess of (Loelia Mary Grosvenor), *Grace and Favour*, Weidenfeld and Nicolson, 1961

Ziegler, Philip, *Melbourne: a Biography of William Lamb, 2nd Viscount Melbourne*, Collins, 1976

Index

218